OUTLAW PILOT

TRUE ADVENTURES

OF

JIMMY "MIDNIGHT" ANDERSON

OUTLAW PILOT

J.F. Anderson
Writer's Den
(604) 248-6130

P.O. Box 147, Parksville, B.C., Canada V9P 1R8

OUTLAW PILOT PRINTS
1st November/93~ 2,500
2nd Spring/94~ 2,500
3rd Fall/94~ 2,500
4th Spring/95~ 4,000
OUTLAW PILOT II
1st December/95~ 4,000

Author at Parksville Beach ~ *Classic Photo by Michele*

OUTLAW PILOT
PUBLISHED BY WRITERS DEN

COPYRIGHT   1993 BY JAMES F. ANDERSON
ALL RIGHTS RESERVED,INCLUDING THE RIGHT TO
REPRODUCE THIS BOOK OR PORTIONS THEREOF IN
ANY FORM.

ANDERSON, JAMES F.,1948-
OUTLAW PILOT
ISBN # 0-9697209-0-4

ILLUSTRATIONS BY LARRY DAVIS, RUBY MORGAN,
CAROL ILOTT AND ROD STEWART.

PROSPECTOR JACK (PROSPECTING THE AKIE) IS A
FICTITIOUS NAME, BUT REAL CHARACTER PERSON.
THESE STORIES ARE BASED ON REAL EVENTS.

PRINTED AND BOUND IN CANADA

CONTENTS

Meet Jimmy 'Midnight' Anderson, the 'OUTLAW PILOT' who will take you on an unbelievable bush pilots ride.

The secret of survival in this profession is how to get out of situations before (and occasionally after) one becomes part of the landscape. Out of the many who became bush pilots in the north, few came through unscathed. Jimmy beat the odds and made it his life.

Scenarios arising from an airplane crash on the icy cold waters of the Akie River, a daring air rescue on the river banks of the Prophet, wildlife capture high on the plateaus of the Tuchodi and Klingzut mountain ranges, and his regular mail deliveries were stories told again and again in his 'bush pilots roost' on Pink Mountain. Stories that legends are made from.

These stories date from the early sixties to the mid seventies. Repeating them is as natural to Jamie as flying is to his father.

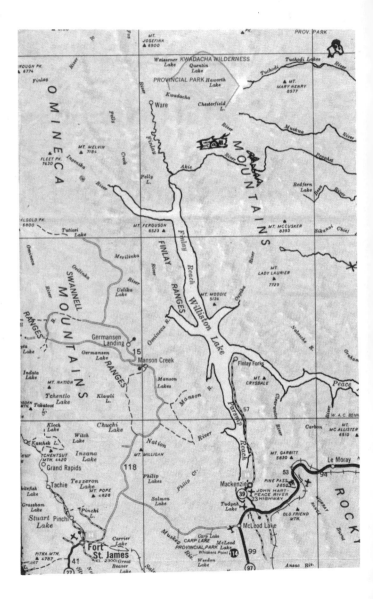

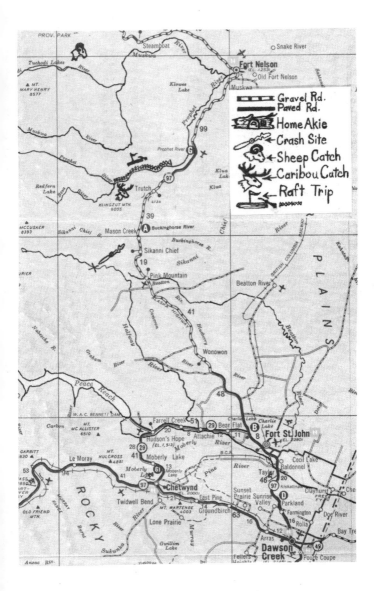

Legend

Gravel Rd.	
Paved Rd.	
Home Akie	
Crash Site	
Sheep Catch	
Caribou Catch	
Raft Trip	

DEDICATED

TO

MY MOTHER, MONA,

WHO HAS ALWAYS BEEN THERE

MY FIRST SHEEP HUNT

I awoke with a start. Ringing, piercing the darkness. My hand automatically reaching out to slap down the alarm button on the Big Ben clock. The hands were straight up and down - 6:00 a.m. - the day had begun. My heart seemed to beat in rhythm with the 30 kilowatt Listor Diesel driven generator that powered my Grandfather's lodge. This was the morning I had been waiting for throughout the Christmas holidays. Today was the start of the journey to Tuchodi Lake hunting territory. My father was to spearhead the first known live capture of Rocky Mountain Stone Sheep. Reaching for my G.W.G blue jeans, I noticed Brian, my buddy from Taylor Flats, was reaching for his glasses on the night table located between the two narrow beds in the small room.

The cook had already started the day. The big wood stove would be fired up downstairs, alleviating the two oil burning heaters that supplemented the warmth of the seventeen room lodge. Slipping my moccasins over my grey wool socks I exclaimed, "Let's go, Buddy... Smell the bacon and eggs." The cafe would be nice and warm as we ate breakfast with my Dad's brother Ben. Ben would be driving us to Trutch Lodge.

It was almost 9:00 a.m. by the time we had driven the rough and narrow snow-covered 53 miles from our place at Pink Mountain, Mile 147 on the Alaska Highway, to Trutch Mountain. Uncle Ben, Brian and I loaded supplies from his new 1963 Ford half ton truck into Al Henderson's Super Cub.

We lifted off from the Trutch airstrip and headed northwest to the Great Rocky Mountain divide. The sun was peaking over the horizon in the east, the first rays of morning made the already bright stars hanging in the sky look like the big lights hung on the Christmas tree we had just left behind. The hum of the aircraft motor, combined with the restless night I had in anticipation of the big day, soon caused me to drift off into a dream-like state, thinking back over the last two weeks of Christmas holidays.

Although I was not eligible for my drivers licence until the end of the month, Brian had his,

JACKPINE SAVAGE

but no 'wheels.' We elected to catch the Greyhound bus from Fort St. John where we both went to school. It had taken about two and a half hours to travel the 100 miles, and we had talked of the possibility of becoming involved in the sheep hunt. It was to take place right after the New Year. We knew we would have to plead with our families to take time off from school. Through the holidays we had helped stock up food and

ME AND AL OEMINGS `PET'

supplies for a two week stay in the mountains, and prepare the ropes and nets we would be using to capture the sheep.

Dad had been informed by Don Peck, the guide and outfitter of the Tuchodi Lake territory that Stone Sheep would travel uphill if chased, so Dad's plan was to go to a high flat peak, and set the nets up in a V-shape, with a rope stretched across the opening. Hanging lariat nooses would be attached with hay wire to the taunt rope, and the ends of the lariats anchored to large rocks. When the sheep were herded through the opening in the V, they would be lassoed by the hung nooses and the 50 to 75 pound rocks would slow down their movement. The ground team would then rush in and hog-tie their feet.

I was visualizing how cramped it would be for a Stone

Sheep in the back of a Super Cub - (as that is where Brian and I were now sitting with supplies packed around us) - when the

BASE CAMP

smooth rumble of the Lycoming motor was suddenly interrupted by a coughing and sputtering. Coming out of my semi-sleeping state I could see a very worried look on Brian's face. Peeking over the front seat passed Al busily flipping switches and through the windshield, I could see us trying to top a high mountain peak. I heard a sigh of relief as we looked down on a small valley about a half mile below. Al dropped the nose of the Super Cub down to pick up air speed and the carburetor de-icer started to thaw the ice that had formed from the high altitude. I didn't drift off again but enjoyed the raw scenery which (although I had seen it many times before flying with Dad) never ceased to fascinate me.

After another twenty minutes of icing and de-icing and a few prayers on my part, we eventually broke through a narrow gap in the mountain range to a large valley that was the bottom end of Tuchodi Lake. Looking down the valley we could see the outline of the log buildings and corrals of Don Peck's base camp.

In a few minutes the skis of Al's Super Cub set down on the horse pasture that had been improvised as a runway, and pulled up to Dad's 150 hp Super cub that was affectionately called Jackpine Savage III. The plane was called this because of the green left on the props from close calls with spruce trees. Dad said he numbered the craft so he could keep track of expenses.

Stopping the cub within a few yards of the main hunting cabin, Dad came walking towards us wearing his old Stetson cowboy hat, the fur-lined collar of his flight jacket pulled up around the back of his neck. His blue jeans were tucked into the top of home made lynx mukluks, protected at the soles by black moccasin rubbers. We swung the plane doors open and Dad, greeting us with a big smile, said, "What took you cowboys so long?"

Al and Dad talked about the flight and checked the carbs, while Brian and I unloaded the plane. Harry Snider, a long-legged cowboy who worked on a regular basis for Dad; and Pete Butler, the Indian cook, packed the supplies into the large cabin.

Sitting around the supper table that night, Dad laid out the final plan for the assault on the mountain the next morning. Al had left to return home soon after he and Dad had ascertained that the carbs were alright. There were five of us left - Dad, Harry, Pete, Brian and myself.

Just as daylight broke, with nine spruce poles two inches in diameter and eight feet long, strapped to the wing strut of the Savage, Dad and Harry lifted off for the summit. The poles would make three sturdy tripods to hold the net, one at each point of the V. The next trip held Peter and Brian. I was to go on the last two trips to air drop the rest of the supplies on Maternity Mountain. The only part of the mountain we could land on was just a few hundred feet long and ended in a sheer drop off almost one mile straight down. Thin air and a heavy load meant landing speed would have to be much higher than usual. The landing gear could be damaged and we always faced the possibility of the skis not slowing us enough before we hit the end of the makeshift runway.

I watched Jackpine Savage swoop out of the clear sky, lower onto the snow-covered pasture and taxi up to the pile of supplies to be dropped onto the summit. The nets were stuffed into gunnysacks. Three of the six sacks were laid on the floor of the Super Cub, the back seat had been taken out to make room for gear and supplies. A ten-gallon drum of aviation gas was placed on top of the sacks and a roll of hay wire was thrown in. This would be used to tie the tripods together and also to hold the lariats in place along the rope stretched across the opening of the V.

I jumped in and sat on the pile. Dad climbed into the pilot's seat, pulled the bottom door flap into place, then tugging the top flap down from the friction fit attachment locked it into place. Fired up the Savage, buckled his seat belt and we were off.

The flight from the cabin to the mountain was about ten minutes. During that time Dad and I went over the way we were going to drop. The first pass we made was at about one hundred feet. I positioned myself on the gas drum, Dad threw open the door flaps of the Super Cub. The twenty-below air rushed into the plane at sixty miles per hour taking my breath away for an instant. Looking out the open door, far below I could see Harry, Brian and Pete. Dad shouted "Drop!" I threw the coil of wire out the door and it whistled through the air to hit ground not twenty feet from Pete. The next drop would be from about fifteen feet as the gas drum could not be dropped from too high or it would split open. I balanced the one hundred pound barrel on the side of the door frame. Dad throttled back and slowed the plane to about thirty miles per hour.

"Now!" Dad said. I toppled the barrel out of the plane, but as I let go of the heavy drum, it did not leave my hand. The wind chill had frozen my leather mitt to the front edge of the metal container and the weight of the gas was pulling me out of the Cub. I tried to stop the momentum of the toppling barrel and sweat popped out on my forehead as I saw the ground flying by at 30 mph. At the last moment my hand slipped out of the mitt and the canister shaped vessel tumbled out of the aircraft and bounced along the mountain top.

After this unpleasant experience. I used a piece of rope to tie myself to the back cross member of the plane. Once again the Savage glided towards the drop site tipped at an angle so that the load would not hit the landing gear and knock a ski off. The simultaneous dropping of the three sacks of rope net on the next pass went a bit smoother. Returning for the rest of the supplies gave me time to improve the hemp tie between my wide leather belt and the Jackpine Savage

I felt a lot more secure dropping the second load of gas and nets with my lifeline securely attached to my waist. Once the drop was complete, Dad and I landed and proceeded to set up the V trap. By nightfall the crew was confident the trap was secure and strong enough to hold the 150 pounds of wild sheep, we were hoping to catch.

In the morning I awoke to the blast of blowing snow crystals coming in the door of the 20 X 30 foot log cabin, as Dad came in brushing the powder snow from his fleece-lined flight jacket. During the night the north wind had blown up a storm, and he had been out checking the tie-downs on the plane.

Doesn't look like we'll be flying today,' he said. "Wind speed is 40 mph and visibility about 200 yards."

For the next two days we played cards and cut firewood. The wood cook stove was the only source of heat in the log cabin. Pete kept the coffee pot full and hot.

On the third morning, much to the excitement of Brian and myself, the wind quit as suddenly as it had started. We knew our week away from school was running out and we wanted to be involved in the catch. The two days of being cooped up was wearing on everyone, and although Pete was a decent cook, bannock and moose steak only went so far.

Harry said one night "Pete, this bannock is too salty, and the steak is over done, but it's the best damn dinner I've had in a long time." The last part was to assure he did not end up chef. The law of the cabin was that anyone complaining of the cooking, would prepare the next meal.

By 10:00 a.m. Dad had everyone hidden behind an outcropping of rocks on the side of the mountain. We watched as Dad made pass after pass over the herd of Mountain Sheep. Persistently trying to drive them from the ravine where they ran to escape the giant metal bird in the sky. After two or three hours of hard flying dad had the sheep on the plateau and was driving the animals towards the net. The plane flew over our heads and the motor was cut.

I could hear Dad's voice, "They're in the opening of the net!.. Herd them in!"

We scrambled out from behind the rocks and climbed up on the top of the mountain. Just in time to see the white tails of three sheep heading over the edge of the plateau. Dad landed shortly after and said, "We'll try again in the morning. The sheep are too panicky to work with and by the time I bring in another herd it will be dark."

That night while sitting around the table drinking a hot buttered rum, (that Dad had a reputation for making), we discussed the problem of concealment. For decent cover, we had to be too far from the net.

The next morning found us all on the mountain lying

covered with white bed sheets, a few yards from the opening of the net. The Jackpine Savage, stripped bare inside except for the pilot's seat and pilot, would have to be fuelled more often today to keep the weight down. Dad was going deeper into the ravines and crevices, weight was critical. Watching with baited breath I heard the plane roaring above the lower peaks and then, nothing for what seemed like an eternity.

Laying on the gunnysacks which protected me from the hard, cold mountain, I visualized Dad throttling back the 150 hp Lycoming and gliding down into the ravine towards the scampering sheep. At the last moment he threw on full power to roar up behind the herd of Stone Sheep, making them race up the mountain side away from this eagle of the mountains, who repeatedly swooped down into their protective crevices.

I remembered a comment Dad had made last night as he jokingly said, "I hope Peck doesn't get upset that we have trained all of his sheep to run downhill into the ravine, instead of up the mountain like he told us they would."

I laid shivering under the white sheet and wondered if it was from the bitter cold, or from the excitement of the moment I could feel was close.

I heard the engine on the flying eagle from the north once again go silent, and 'Midnight' Anderson from high above hollered out in a calm clear voice, "O.K. guys, they're in the opening, let's get them!"

I threw the sheet from my body and jumped up running for the opening of the net. Pete and I were on the west side of the trap and Harry and Brian were on the east side. I saw two sheep nervously prancing across the opening of the 'V'. Only a few feet from the dangling nooses.

Harry and Brian came running from the east side of the trap, turning the sheep towards Pete and I. At a dead run I angled to head the pair off as they started to trot north away from the V. I knew if we didn't get one today, the old man would be choked. The first sheep, a young ram, whistled by me. With freezing air biting at my lungs, I rushed out to jump in front of a big ewe, turning her back toward Pete who waved his arms and yelled, turning her right into the net.

She did not even see or feel the lariat as the Mountain Sheep rushed headlong towards the back of the 'V'. When she hit the end of the 50 feet of rope attached to the seventy-five pound rock, the hemp leash jerked back and threw her to the ground. Within moments the ewe was subdued. We walked her over to the mountain airstrip where the Super Cub was already landing. It was quickly decided that the female sheep would be flown to the cabin while still in a state of shock. The sheep was then wrapped in a tarp and loaded into the Savage, I jumped in on top of the bound animal to keep her calm. "It's probably her first plane ride so she might be a bit nervous." said Dad.

The northern aviator would bring the rest of the crew down from Maternity mountain next trip. Pete, being the

smallest, was placed way in the back behind the cross member, that Brian would sit on as far back as he could, long tall Harry squeezed into the rest of the space. Dad pulled his pilot's seat forward to make the extra room needed. Weight on take-off was not too vital on the mountain because at the end of the short strip was the sheer drop, and as long as the cub had enough speed to clear the first rock outcropping about fifty feet down, the plane would pick up all the air speed it needed as it glided under full power down the mountain side. The first couple of times we took off this way

gave me a queasy feeling in my stomach. But as Dad explained, the updraft on the side of the mountain combined with all the airspeed he wanted gave the cub a lot of lift and was one of the easiest take-offs he made.

In the morning Brian and I would be heading back. The cub had burned up more fuel than expected, and Dad had to fly into 147 to pick up another two drums of aviation gas.

Dad figured with the one drum left at base camp minus the three gallons of av gas needed to supplement the flight to

147. Plus the twenty gallons returning, there would be twenty-seven gallons of drummed fuel. Combined with full wing tanks on the return trip, enough fuel for several days herding. 'I had better bring back some extra grub we could be here awhile.' It was then that Harry said, "What drum, Jim? We used up the last of the gas today!"

Cold realization that Harry was right, dawned on the whole camp the next morning, when we finished counting the empty drums. We were sixty miles from the nearest settlement, and the only other way out besides aircraft was to walk, or capture the free roaming half-wild saddle ponies that Don Peck had used in the fall hunt. It was starting to look like Brian and I were to miss more school.

"There has had to be gas here some place, for that tractor and cat that Peck walked in during the summer" said Dad. We searched every nook and cranny for gas, but could not find any.

"Jim, that would be ordinary purple farm gas used in those machines." Harry said. "It would never get that aircraft off the ground." Dad replied, "I have enough av gas in the right wing tank to take off and land with. Once we are in the air I could switch tanks and use the farm gas." That's when it dawned on me! "There is probably gas left in the tractor and cat. We could drain that, couldn't we?" "Good idea!" exclaimed Dad, "Let's check it out." We found half a barrel of gas in the two pieces of equipment. Dad poured the purple fuel twice through an old felt hat he had just for straining contaminated gas.

We arrived at 147 later that afternoon to spread the good news. The stone sheep would be kept at base camp in one of the smaller log cabins, until it was not as spooky, so that the long flight from Tuchodi, to Mile 147, would not over stress the animal.

The next day, Brian and I caught the bus back to Fort St. John. I left the lodge with regret. I would no longer be involved in the Rocky Mountain Sheep hunt. But I had some satisfaction in knowing I would be back at the lodge next weekend and would have lots of opportunities to be with the Rocky Mountain Stone Sheep that would eventually be caught and flown to 147 where they would be held in a log barn until all seven Stone Sheep could be shipped by truck to Al Oeming's game farm outside of Edmonton, Alberta.

MAIL DROP

*I*t was early Spring. I looked out of the front window of the family lodge. Just past the gas pumps an 18-wheeler was smoothly shifted into gear, pulling away to continue its journey to points north. The freight liner moved slowly onto the muddy highway exposing a view of tall spruce surrounding a snow and ice covered marsh. I could also now see the 147 mile post. This post marked the distance from Dawson Creek, mile zero of the Alaska Highway.

FAMILY EATING NOOK

Glancing up I saw white patches of snow fall from the large spruce trees, creating mini avalanches as the warm Chinook winds turned the crystal-like powder into heavy soft tumbling mounds. The falling clumps landing onto the lower snow covered evergreen branches added weight to the already sagging branches and would cause the whole tree to shudder and turn from white to green in a matter of seconds, the cascading snow pounding down onto the frozen earth.

I was finishing a late Saturday breakfast when Dad came in through the doors of the cafe, removing his mud-covered rubbers from his moccasins.

CUB OUTFITTED WITH SKIS

"Eat up and give me a hand with these supplies," said Dad. "We have a mail drop over in the Half Way Valley and then we will circle on back to 147, fuel up and load the cargo for Donny's base camp. The way this Chinook is coming in it could be our last trip with just skis. It's getting awfully soft out there."

I was no stranger to the mail drop. It was almost commonplace in the Spring and Fall when the road from Mile 143 to the Halfway Valley was transforming from the frost-hard of Winter to the sun-dried way of Summer. The valley access turned to a slippery, muddy gumbo. Unless it was a pressing matter people just never left their homesteads.

If there was urgent mail or messages, Dad would lift off from Sikanni Chief flight strip and fly back into the Halfway Valley to do a mail drop before he continued on his flight plan. He would throttle back on the engine and glide in over the log buildings. Just as the tips of the landing skis attached to the super cub were about to touch the shingled roof, he would slam the throttle full forward and the 150 hp Lycoming motor would roar to life as it pulled Jackpine Savage back into the sky, giving Dad enough altitude for another pass. By this time the family that he 'buzzed' had gathered their faculties that had been

FILL UP

temporarily lost as their life went from absolute quiet existence (other than possibly a radio trying painfully to pick up reception in a far corner of the room), to an earth-shattering window-shaking roar. Realizing that Jimmy 'Midnight' Anderson was outside and being as the fields were too soft to land on, they knew he would be dropping something and would venture out to receive the tidings.

    When Dad came back for a second pass, an envelope or small package would come fluttering through the air with about three feet of red survey ribbon attached. The receivers could be rest assured that the package would land not far from where they stood. The one setback was if they were too close to the cabin a misguided air drop could end up on the roof.

I recall the time we were dropping a fly-by message to a valley rancher who was peacefully ploughing his fields with his Case tractor. He never had a chance to see us. With the engine cut, Dad glided down from 1,000 feet. Just as Dad and the northern cattleman had eye contact, the Lycoming roared to life. By the time the isolated rancher had recovered from our first pass and shut his tractor off, the message was fluttering through the air. I watched from the back seat of the super cub. The machine operator kept his eye on the red ribbon, not knowing which way to go if he left the tractor. Finally he reached out and snatched the message from the air.

I could never figure out whether Dad got a bigger charge out of a perfect drop or the visible jump of the peaceful homesteader, when the Savage came to life.

GRIZZLY STORIES & ROCKY MOUNTAIN SHEEPBURGERS

Wing tanks refreshed and cargo for a passenger seat, the Savage lifted off from Sikanni Chief flight strip and headed northwest towards a camp nestled on the shores of the Sikanni River. I had never been to Don Beattie's base camp before. Used for hunting mountain sheep in the early winter months and in the spring grizzly bear, the cabin was strategically located in the guide's territory .

Arriving a week earlier by horseback, the supplies Don and the guides had brought with them were now getting a little stale. Arrangements had been made with Dad to bring in fresh grub and mail from my Grandfather's general store and post office.

The outfitter was repairing winter damage and rounding up and re-breaking the half wild pack horses used in last falls' sheep hunt. American hunters would soon be arriving at the start of the spring season to bag a trophy grizzly.

We "buzzed" the cabin. Don and two guides came out. The second pass Dad flew low over the pasture to check out the snow conditions. " It's too soft to land." he said. "One ski could get bogged down and flip us. We'll check out the river." We circled back behind the cabin and flew low over the tributary. I could tell at first glance there was no way we were going to land on the Sikanni. Less than 100 feet wide, the river would have been a great landing strip in the dead of winter when it was covered over with thick ice. However the early spring chinook had melted snow from the sun baked mountains releasing many thousand rivulets of sparkling liquids rushing to the river system. Ice extending 25 feet from each shore strained as a freshet of water forty feet wide flowed over the ice and moved freely down the middle of the frozen watercourse.

I tapped the old man on the shoulder and said, "Dad, we're going to have to drop these supplies. There is no way we are going to land on that river with skis on the bottom of the Savage."

"We've got some valuable cargo on board and we're not packed for an air drop" said Dad. "Don and the boys would be peeved if that Jack Daniel medicine happened to get broken in the drop. We'll have to land on the river."

I figured the old man was putting the kid on, so I sort of smiled and sat back in my seat, a little disappointed that we were turning around and heading back to 147. The disappointment was two-fold. I figured being a young lad of 17 in the woods with hunters and bush pilots should make for some good stories and there would be a better than equal chance that I could sample a little of that medicine, with Dad and the guys.

I soon realized we were not heading home but circling back over the cabin. From my cargo seat I looked past the spinning prop as the Savage finished it's circle. To my dismay I could see the outstretched arms of the Sikanni and impending doom. Dad nosed the aircraft down, skimed along the water, then touched the skis to the river. Dad levelled the Savage out. Much to my surprise the skis reacted to the river like that of a water skier. Our landing speed of 60 knots lowered to about 30 knots. Wing flaps still lowered to keep the aircraft as light as possible, we momentarily cruised the tributary until we came upon a large piece of ice protruding down into the water from the snow covered river bank. Using the tail rudder for steering, the Savage seemed to hop from the water onto the submerged

sheet of ice. Dad immediately throttled down on the big
Lycoming and the Savage picked it's way along the icy edge of
the brush and treed banks bordering the Sikanni. Soon we came
to a cleared piece on the river that Don's horses used to come
down to drink. Skiing up to the sloped bank, the throttle was
eased forward and the big work prop pulled the Savage up the
incline onto the pasture we had just checked for snow conditions
not 50 feet from Don Beattie's cabin.

There was a festive atmosphere as the supplies were
broken open. Hunting and flying stories flowed freely. A quart
jar of canned meat was brought up from the root cellar and we
downed the best Rocky Mountain sheep burgers I had ever
tasted.

Time flew by. All too soon Dad was looking out the
cabin door to see if the heat had gone out of the sun. The snow
in the pasture would soon start to crystallize. I had talked to Dad
about taking off. I didn't want any more river surprises. He
assured me we would not be using the Sikanni as a flight strip to
leave on.

"What we'll do," he said, "is make several back and
forth passes on the pasture and pack down a strip of snow so the
skis will slide smooth and free."

Wing tips almost touching the snow the Jackpine Savage
struggled down the pasture. First one ski and then another broke
through the crusty cover. Wings dipping from side to side, like a
wounded spruce hen struggling through the forest, the Savage
broke track to the base of the horse pasture. Limping back
towards the cabin after a large 180 degree turn, the Savage set
the already well marked ski trail.

On the second pass I jumped in the back for weight.
Once again the Savage struggled down the pasture, smoothing
the make shift runway.

Returning from the third pass the Savage cruised along

with hardly a bump. Turning the cub around and nosing into the wind, the throttle was thrust forward. The 150 hp Lycoming roared into action, and slipping down the runway the tail-section lifted on the Savage.

We gathered more speed, but I knew the Savage would not be airborne before we reached the end of the strip. There stood two towering spruce trees 100 feet high and spaced about 60 feet apart. Their branches straining to connect the two giants. I could see that even if we did get airborne, those two spruce would rip the wings from the Savage, sending the fuselage like a broken arrow onto the frozen muskeg.

A sigh of relief escaped my lips as Dad throttled back on the Lycoming. The tail of the cub dropped and we circled once more and travelled the well packed ski trail back to the cabin.

I saw our dilemma. The snow covering the short strip was not good enough to take off on. Large boulders frozen into the icy river banks prevented the build up of enough speed to ski from land onto the water. The river was definitely out of the question.

I knew Dad was flying out today and I was curious - very curious - as to how we were to get the Savage back into the air. Dad did a 180 in front of the cabin and pulled his side window open. Don came up along the side of the plane and asked, "Have you enough strip?"

Dad responded, "If you and the boys give me a hand!"

"What can we do Jim?"

With a man on each wing strut Don grabbed the lift handles on the aircraft tail. Pushing against the metal struts connecting the wing to the body of the Savage, the men moved the airplane back to the end of the strip with the tail section almost to the front door of the log cabin. The guides then ducked under the strut and hung on from behind, far enough out on the wing strut so the leading edge of the tail section would miss them, when the Savage took off.

Dad eased the throttle forward. The 150 hp Lycoming built up rpm's. The Savage began to shake and prance like a stallion race horse at the starting gate, gradually pulling the men a few feet as the prop of the powerful Lycoming blew crystal flakes of snow in it's wake. Dad closed the sliding window and nodded to Don who was standing 30 feet in front and a little to the left of the plane. Don dropped the arm holding his hat and the two men released the aircraft simultaneously.

The Savage leaped from its starting harness and raced down the well-worn ski trail. Within a few yards the tail section came up and the cub steadily picked up take-off speed until the headwinds gently picked the aircraft's wings into the air. The cub picked up air speed but not enough altitude to clear the tops of the two deadly spruce at the end of the runway.

Reaching the end of the runway with a 70 foot elevation, I braced myself for the impact of wings being ripped from the belly of the aircraft. Moments from contact, the Savage dropped its starboard wing. Maneuvering the craft into a hard right bank, Dad had put the wings into a straight up and down position, leaving lots of air space on either side of the Savage's cockpit, for the future growth of the ancient spruce.

Once the 'G' forces allowed me to move again, I leaned forward and listened over the drone of the wind and engine while Dad explained; that when he put the plane into a hard bank, under full throttle and then pulled back on the joystick, the air current hitting the belly of the aircraft, gave the same cylinder effect of a motorcycle climbing the interior of a huge barrel. In this case the cylinder effect came from the air itself giving even more lift to the uncanny air design of the Super Cub.

I settled back in my seat for the flight home, and a wave of euphoria flowed through my body. I thought of all the stories I had heard of how the tips of the Jackpine Savage prop became green, and decided I would never doubt another tale.

Authors
Grandparents
Jim and Lila
Anderson
in front of
Pink Mountain
General Store

LONG FLIGHT HOME

*T*he sound of the alternate coughing and high engine rev of an aircraft motor was the first audible sign of trouble. The Super Cub burst through the cloud formation not yet dissipated by the cold front that had just moved into the upper Halfway Valley.

If there had been an observer in this isolated part of northeastern British Columbia, they would have seen the steep bank of the craft, as it seemed to line up for a landing on a rather open part of the wide rocky banks of the Halfway River. The pilot had cut what power the airplane had left and was coming in low over the bank, the craft twisted and turned between the larger poplar trees that grew beside the river. At thirty feet above the water, it glided towards the smoothest part of the improvised landing strip, which was covered in a scattering of boulders and young poplar trees.

Jackpine Savage III had been affectionately painted on the nose of the aircraft by the pilot Jimmy 'Midnight' Anderson, who was now gliding the cub between large rocks looking for the best part of the small stretch of bank to land. When the over-sized bush tires touched the uneven ground, it looked as if this landing was destined to be a rough one. Jim yanked back on the joystick to lift the right wheel of the Savage over a large boulder, the aircraft veered to the left turning it toward a large mass of driftwood, piled high against the bank through years of spring run-off.

The pilot immediately threw the controls into a hard right, away from a sure crackup. The lowered right wing hit a young poplar tree that a moment ago would have slapped the leading edge, and bent as the wing passed over it. However, banked at this wild angle, the starboard wing hit the sapling

JACKPINE SAVAGE

three feet lower snapping the trunk of the young tree. It's jagged edges ripped into the aircraft fabric hooking into the wing frame. This caused the almost stopped plane to pause in mid-air, turn slightly and come down hard on the landing gear. Sending rocks the size of oranges flying through the air, the idling work prop dug into the hard river bed, bringing the Jackpine Savage to a complete rest.

Earlier in the day, George Ross an old-time friend, had stopped at my father and uncle's lodge at Mile 147 on the Alaska Highway for lunch and a visit. He and Dad had decided to fly back to the Halfway Valley and check out an old fishing hole.

On their way back to `147' the carb on the Lycoming had started to act up. After a few trying minutes of de-icing the carb, Jimmy had turned around with a concerned smile and said, "Hang on Buds, we're going to have to set the Savage down here. I can't clear the carburettor." George braced for a rough landing.

On impact George was thrown forward into the back of the pilot's seat. Dazed for a moment, he clicked open his seat belt and checked to see how Jimmy was doing. He could see the cracked windshield bulging out from the aircraft, When Jimmy lifted his head, George could see at a glance the blood stained, dash mounted compass, was the cause of the long gash extending from the pilot's forehead, down the side of his nose onto the split cheek. Using a combination of ice cold water from the Halfway river, and five butterfly bandages from the first aid kit (kept under the pilot seat), George managed to stop the bleeding.

Once Jimmy's wound had been attended, they walked around the aircraft to survey the damage. The wing structure had been badly damaged from the broken poplar. The prop was pitted and curled on the ends from digging into the river bed. The undercarriage was practically ripped off from the last contact it had with the earth. The windshield, although still in one piece, was covered with spider webbed cracks, which had allowed it to bulge out of the frame about six inches.

George surveyed the mess. He looked at Jimmy and said, "Well Midnight, that was one hell of a crash."

The veteran pilot looked back at George with a smile on his cut up face, and a devil-may-care glint in his eye, "Hell Buds, you don't walk away from a crash - that was a landing, and just as sure as Christ was a cowboy, we'll be flying her out of here."

Two days later saw us packing supplies down the bank that Dad and George had climbed out of. This time a trail had been blazed out by Indian cook Pete Butler. A supply of food, tents and sleeping bags were brought in by my dad's brother Ben, Harry Snyder, a tall cowboy that worked for Dad; myself, a friend Johnny Charette, and of course Dad and George. Next, oxygen and acetylene tanks were wrestled through the woods along with the several hand tools and material we would need for the restoration of Jackpine Savage III.

Setting up camp and clearing a working area around the plane kept Pete and Dad busy, while the rest of the crew brought in the last of the supplies. The two mile hike through the forest made the packing of supplies difficult. Each trip however would make the

ANDERSON'S LODGE, MILE 147, ALASKA HIGHWAY

pathway more accessible. The first trail improvement was falling a dead snag across a patch of impassable muskeg. The limbless bridge eliminated a quarter mile detour around the mossy bog, making the last half of the mosquito infested trek substantially shorter.

With trail improvements finished, the last convoy of tools included an immense anvil strapped to the back of my uncle Ben. The rugged trail began with a sharp incline down off the Halfway Valley roadway. Navigating through various gullies and steep terrain, the trail meandered down to the flattened drainage of the lowland.

We left Ben at a hastily built rest stop, fashioned (with a chain saw brought in on a previous trip) out of a wind fallen log lying along the pathway. From here my uncle would not need the assistance of the rest of the packers.

The maneuvering of the cumbersome anvil would be less than on the mountain side. Not wanting to hold up the crew, Ben elected to follow up the rear for the last half of the walk and meet everyone at the site. Once the smoke break was over, we re-strapped the heavy anvil to his back and headed out towards camp. Ben gamely trudging after.

It had been a real job getting the 80 lb. anvil to the valley floor, but now the travelling was relatively easy. Ben felt the tug of the ropes biting into his shoulder muscles, the weight of the anvil driving his footprints into the soft trail, occasionally leaving moisture to come rushing into the deep imprints of the square boot heel.

With the confidence of an experienced woodsman, Ben carefully stepped on the log. The long slender tree was not a wide path, but the fifty foot bridge was still a lot more attractive than the mushy walk around the bug and moss infested marsh.

Looking up to see the end not 20 feet away, Ben failed to notice the small piece of moss on the river side of a slight knot, protruding from the old log. A heavy western work boot came down on the slimy vegetation causing Ben to momentarily lose balance. The bulk of the massive anvil pulled him over backwards to go 'splat' into the muskeg. The block of iron sunk into the bog tugging at the rope harness, holding Ben's body steadfast in the sucking substance.

Reaching for his knife belted above the right hip pocket of his Levis, Ben put weight on his right leg to lift the submerged hip, and caused his right foot to immediately sink in the northern muskeg. Carefully, to avoid sinking any further, Ben reached into his right front pocket to procure his Zippo lighter.

Burning through the sweat dampened 3/8 inch hemp with the flame of the reliable torch proved to be fruitless and became unbearably hot through Ben's sweat moistened denim shirt, before doing any substantial damage to the rope holding the anvil to his back.

Struggling was useless, movement seemed to only sink the anvil bearing body further into the mire. Easing cigarettes from the left breast pocket and lighting up a Players, Ben relaxed his exhausted iron clad frame and blew smoke at the circling insects. Hoping that Jimmy would send out a search party before the mosquitos ate too much of him, or the constant tug of the muskeg covered anvil sucked him under.

The search was completed some fifteen minutes after Dad decided Ben was long over due. Finding him pinned to the grimy ground when we arrived on the scene, Dad asked if he was all right. In good spirits, Ben started razing Dad about taking so long to come looking for him.

Not a wise thing to do! A smile crossed the weather beaten face of the bush pilot. He sat down on the log and lighting up a smoke, started talking about stepping on his younger brothers chest to see how long it would take for him to sink out of sight. The raillery went on until the cigarette was finished.

By this time the jargon response coming from the larger of

my Grandfathers two sons, was turning into threats and scenarios of what he would do with the discarded remains of his older brother, once he did get up.

Sensing the joviality rapidly diminishing, and with an airplane waiting to be rebuilt, Dad reached for his buck pathfinder knife, and in one movement touched it to the straining 3/8 inch rope. Immediately releasing my slightly ruffled, but grateful uncle, from the seizing swamp.

Dragging the anvil up from the depths of the sucking mire was a feat in itself. Once out of the muskeg, Ben insisted he carry the badly needed slime infested heavy iron block to camp. His already muck moisten back would not get any dirtier. He started packing that S.O.B. in, and by God he'd finish.

With eyes twinkling under the brim of the old stetson hat, the north woods bush pilot looked his younger brother in the eye, " If that's the way you want it Buds, that's how she'll be". With that we hiked the short distance back to camp, the anvil again roped to the wide back of my uncle Ben.

The next week saw a beehive of activity on the river bank of the isolated Halfway River. By using long poles cut from surrounding woods, and with the use of leverage, the aircraft was blocked up and braced. The prop and landing gear were removed, and the windshield was pushed back into the frame. Masking tape was used both on the inside, and outside of the thin plexiglass to hold it in place. The damaged wing membranes were exposed, the broken splintered pieces removed and replaced with buck brush (a local willow). This was run past either side of the hole and haywired to the intact part of the wing. Bed sheets were stretched and glued over the hole and then painted with Aircraft dope. When dry, this liquid substance made the bed sheet drum tight.

The landing gear was disassembled and using heat, it was straightened and brazed together. Bed sheet once again took the place of Aircraft fabric, as it was pulled over the newly rebuilt frame. The fabric dope stretched the bed sheet and two coats of red fabric paint carefully applied, gave the landing gear the look of a factory finished product.

First heated, then placed on the iron block, the damaged prop was straightened by hardy blows from a six lb. sledge hammer, welded by the keen hands of the versed bush pilot. The ends were then filed smooth, and the balanced prop was carefully attached to the front end of the big Lycoming motor.

Dad then removed the carburetor and overhauled the faulty float. The oil was changed and the motor checked over carefully. Dad then attached the battery cable that had been disconnected the day he walked away from the 'landing site'.

The moment had finally arrived. Dad primed the carb of the Savage and hit the ignition. The 150 Lycoming, without as much as a sputter, kicked into a nice even rpm. Easing the throttle forward dad taxied out onto the newly built runway, that Johnny and I had (between other jobs) constructed. We had made the runway as smooth and long as possible by removing trees, and rolling large boulders from a 12 foot wide pathway. Dad had pointed out that if the Savage would not lift off because of some undetectable damage, the aircraft would need some strip to come back down on.

After checking the gauges, Dad pulled the top section of cockpit door close. Shoving the throttle full forward, the Savage raced down the runway with the 150 Lycoming at maximum rpm's. As the cub steadily climbed into the sky, I thought of Dad's words just before he got into the aircraft. "This flight has taken a little longer than usual," he said. "I know the plane is in good shape, but the Savage and I are going to take the last leg solo. I'll see you at the lodge."

By the time we walked the two miles back to the already loaded trucks and drove the twenty-five miles of Halfway Valley road to the lodge, the old man had already a couple cups of coffee under his belt, and had asked the cook to dig out seven of the biggest steaks she could find. The Jackpine Savage had finished the long flight home.

Some three months later, while glancing at the latest copy of the Fort St. John Alaska Hi-way News, there on the front page was a little clip that said Jimmy Anderson had been fined $100.00 for flying aircraft CF-LVR with makeshift parts. I had to smile and shake my head as I thought, "What in the hell does it take to change the old habits of a northern bush pilot?"

A MAN AND HIS CARIBOU

*I*t was late afternoon on a September day and the super cub lifted off from the home-made flight strip on top of Klingzut Mountain. The plane was gaining altitude and off to the east the pilot, Jimmy Anderson, could see Trutch Mountain. Looking southeast, towards his destination of 50 air miles, he saw a low blanket of mist forming over Mile 147 which was where the Beaton River flowed beneath the Alaska Highway. Undaunted, he set his flight course for the Beaton River Lodge, hoping to find a hole in the ground cover. He would then fly at tree-top level until he could land at Sikanni Chief flight strip, not a mile from the Lodge. In a large log barn out back he would deposit his cargo.

A movement in the back of the super cub brought a satisfied smile to his weather-beaten face. He thought back to the first conversation with Leo Rutledge, about his latest contract with Al Oeming, owner of The Alberta Game Farm. Leo had said, "Jimmy, you know I don't mind you using my hunting territory, to live trap a caribou - and to my knowledge it's never been done - but if you do catch any, how are you going to get them off of Klingzut Mountain and then through the 20 some miles of muskeg before you can get to a road?

While Jimmy did his pre-flight inspection on Jackpine Savage, he had explained to Leo how he would remove the back seat from the super cub. Then laying a 2" foam on the floor to stop unnecessary wear on the animal's hide, the caribou would be tied securely and wrapped in a tarp for the one-half to three-quarter hour flight from Klingzut, to Jimmy's hunting lodge located at Mile 147 on the Alaska Highway.

Twenty-one caribou removed from Klingzut Mountain would not hurt the large herds that roamed freely throughout

KLINGZUT MOUNTAIN HEADQUARTERS

the territory Leo hunted. He watched as Jimmy climbed into the cub and fired up the 150 hp Lycoming, and within a couple of hundred feet, lifted the Savage from the pasture strip he used to land on when he dropped in to visit.

Leo smiled and leaned back into his arm chair as he looked out of the window of his comfortable log home. He could see the powerful waters of the Peace River race past the fence of lodge pole pine perched on the banks of the mighty river. He knew Jimmy was a serious young man. If he set his mind to capturing twenty-one caribou with his Jackpine Savage, he more than likely would.

Leo had shaken Jimmy's hand and indicated he would be stopping at Anderson's Lodge on his way to and from his base camp to discuss the type of terrain on the Klingzut Mountain. An experiment crossing large wild caribou with domesticated Canadian Reindeer interested Leo. The project hopefully would produce a larger hybrid reindeer for meat utilization in the Arctic. Many late nights Leo Rutledge would

FATHER(MIDNIGHT ANDERSON), SON, AND CARIBOU

spend at Mile 147 discussing with Jimmy, the caribou ways.

A frown creased Jimmy's face as he circled, looking for an opening in the cloud. He knew the Lodge was under him but could tell from his altimeter that the fog was too close to go through to try and land, so he headed north towards Trutch Mountain. He would try to land on the strip there.

More movement in the back - he turned around to check his cargo and gently fondled the ears of the big four-year-old bull caribou. The animal had been in the back of the cub for well over an hour. Flight time had been extended by half an hour while dipping and diving trying to find an opening. The 400 pound caribou would soon be starting to stiffen up and the aircraft was running low on fuel. The extra weight of the bull meant that the Jackpine Savage had been fuelled lightly to keep down take-off weight due to the low atmosphere of Klingzut Mountain.

DETAINED WILDLIFE

Cold steel strained against my muscles. The three foot handle pumped gas from the underground storage tank up to the top of the old gravity-fed pump. I was wondering when my Dad and Uncle would retire the antiquated machine for a new one. The second dispenser on the gas island served regular gas and was run by an electric pump powered by the diesel generator behind our Lodge. Just as the ten gallon glass bowl above the mint museum piece was again full, I heard the rev of the Lycoming as it made a pass above the fog that had rolled in rather quickly for this time of year. At once I realized Dad would be in trouble. There would be no way he could land the Savage in this soup.

The haze was getting heavier and daylight was starting to run out. Jimmy spotted an opening in the fog, and he instantly nosed the Jackpine Savage towards the top of the tall spruce he could barely see. The Savage burst through the fog cloud and levelled out not 50 feet above the timber to see a short open stretch of highway. Jimmy knew he could not follow the highway because the fog was rolling in quickly and would soon cover even this small opening. There was no other choice - use the Alaska Highway as a landing strip. He could tell at a glance he was at Mile 187 not 13 miles from Trutch Lodge.

The cub touched down and taxied off to the side of the road where the Highways Department had been digging gravel out of the side hill, leaving a flat area just large enough for the wing span of the aircraft to be off the highway.

A Cadillac pulled over to the side of the road. The driver was sure he had seen an aircraft land on the roadway, but, in this fog, it could have been the lights of one of those big freight liners coming at him out of the semi-darkness. Joe was headed back down the Alcan Highway from his holiday to Anchorage. Experience dictated that he slow down and pull over when these bright lights came at him through the fog or dust. It didn't seem to matter how much screen one put in front of the caddy, the rocks flying from truck tires would invariably strike the car some where. Pulling up to where he could see the lights more clearly, he saw the Super Cub sitting in the small gravel pit. Joe noticed the blue jeans, flight jacket and battered cowboy hat, as the pilot climbed out of the aircraft.

The pilot walked over to the car, Joe touched the button

on the door and his window slid down into the side door panel.

"What can we do for you?" He asked, as the friendly face drew closer.

CARIBOU HOSTEL

"Well, this fog has forced me down here. Would you mind stopping at Mile 147 to let everyone know I am O.K.? " asked Jimmy, "And if you have a few minutes, I really would appreciate it if you boys would give me a hand exercising my caribou."

"Your caribou?" questioned Joe

"Yes, that poor animal has been tied up inside the Savage for almost two hours now and I'm worried about the circulation in his legs."

Joe and his partner took another look towards the aircraft just as the big bull raised its head. Involuntarily Joe's finger hit

the button and automatically the window slid halfway up.
Quietly, with eyes bigger than usual he said, "Listen cowboy, I
don't mind delivering your message to 147, but there is no way I
am going to help you exercise your caribou!" With that he was
on his way.

It was about ten minutes after the Caddy had left that a
truck driver pulled his rig over. He had seen the Savage and the
familiar figure of Jimmy Anderson on the side of the road.
Jimmy explained the situation to the line driver, and asked him
to stop at Trutch Lodge to ask Don Peck if he and another hand
could come down and help him with the caribou.

Within an hour Bud Armstrong and friend pulled up in a
Dodge panel truck. Bud said Don was out at his Tuchodi Lake
Hunting Camp for a couple of weeks but they would be happy to
give him a hand.

It was well after dark when Dad came rolling into the
Lodge to get me and my Uncle Ben to help him unload the
caribou from Bud's truck and into the barn. This was a tricky
operation as we already had three caribou waiting inside for
transport to the Alberta Game Farm. When the door to the barn
was opened, occasionally one would try to get out.

With the headlights of the van shining past the barn door,
Bud's friend went in to shoo the other caribou into a far stall.

We hauled the big animal out of the panel truck, and
with Dad holding onto the rope of the horse halter that was on
the bull, we shoved him through the door of the barn. However,
the caribou had other ideas.

Only three days ago, this wild animal had been chased by
a loud gigantic bird that had herded him into a rope snare. Three
cowboys by the names of Harry Snider, Rocky Peck and Sid
Westergard had then hauled him up to the stone hut they had
built for shelter on Klingzut Mountain, where he had been
tethered for two days. Suddenly he had been wrestled down, tied

ROCKYPECK BABY-SITTING CARIBOU
MIDNIGHT - A GREAT PILOT BUT LOUSY BABY-SITTER

up and thrown into a cramped Super Cub for a two-hour flight
of ups and downs. Then dragged from the plane into a dusty
Dodge van for another hour of a rough, twisting ride. Now four

guys were trying to push him into a strange dark building.

With a decision as quick as only a caribou can make, he turned around and headed straight for us and the headlights of the panel truck. As he tried to streak by us, it was natural instinct to grab onto his neck and hang on. I had been around animals - wild and domesticated - all my life but had never felt the power that was coming from this creature. Just as I was reconsidering my rash actions, I felt the body weight of Dad and my broad-shouldered Uncle Ben as we brought the frightened animal down. This time we were more careful as we guided the subdued bull into what would be his home for about a week, until we had enough caribou to make a transport to the game farm.

Later that night, drinking a cup of coffee with just a touch of mix, I could feel the aches and pains from my brief encounter with the legs and hoofs of the Klingzut-raised beast. I thought of earlier in the evening when the new '64 road-beaten Caddy had pulled up to the pumps and the driver had said, "Is this Anderson's Lodge?"

"Yes it is," I said. "What can we do for you?"

The driver, a bewildered look still in his eyes, said, "I have a message for you, . . . from a man and his caribou."

GRANDAD ANDERSON MOUNTED ON ONE OF HIS EVER CHANGING RODEO STOCK

WINGS ON THE PROPHET

'**W**ilderness experience' jumped from the telegram received by Pat Crofton who was stationed at B.C. House, in London, England. Victoria's Department of Travel had decided to invite a number of the media from Europe, the United States, United Kingdom, Japan, and eastern Canada, (with the cooperation of Canadian Pacific Airways) to northeastern B.C. and the Peace River country. Pat's position as Director of Travel Promotion for British Columbia, made him a prime candidate for this group who were to be exposed to the Canadian North, for a true wilderness adventure. The exposition was put together locally by the associated Chamber of Commerce (parent body of the Peace River Alaska Highway Tourist Association). The tourist coordinator was Earl Hanson.

TOURING

First stop on the tour was Dawson Creek, 'Mile Zero' on the Alaska Highway. A reception and dinner at the Park Hotel offered an opportunity to introduce Pat, along with the other thirty-nine writers of the International press tour, to some of the local people.

The next morning the group was given a tour through the farming and lumber community of Chetwynd and were treated to huge barbecued T-bone steaks at Moberley Lake. The tour was then taken for a drive through quaint Hudson's Hope to visit the W.A.C. Bennett Dam. Lake Williston the largest body of inland water in B.C. was created by the dam regulating the flow of the once wild and mighty Peace river.

The expedition of the northern communities finished with a closing banquet at the Alexander MacKenzie Inn, Fort

St. John. Located at Mile 47 on the two lane roadway
stretching 1,523 miles from Dawson Creek to Fairbanks,
Alaska, the inn's name reflects some of the oldest and richest
history of the northernmost of the four communities.

THE NEXT DAY

On June 4, 1975 the party of 40 writers split into three
groups for mini wilderness tours from Fort St. John. One
group elected to spend the night at a fishing camp. They
received a fly-in view of the Rockies, then landed on a small
lake teeming with rainbow trout. The second group chose a
river boat ride up the Peace River to the W.A.C. Bennett Dam.
An over night camp and fishing, highlighted the trip. Both
expeditions went off without a hitch.

The third group elected to go on a motorcade up the
Alaska Highway and embark on a tour that was offered by
Horst Breithaupt of Wilderness Lodge, at mile 200 on the
Alaska Highway. The adventure was to provide a 'taste of the
wilderness,' for this group of city writers from foreign
countries. Keeping in mind these reporters were not adventure
seekers out for a thrill, the trip had been designed for the
proverbial little old lady in tennis shoes.

The day was bright and the ride smooth until Mile 83
where the paved road turned to gravel. From here the last link
of the international road system running from Buenos Aires
Argentina, to Fairbanks Alaska, would be a twisting, turning
gravel thoroughfare, transforming the pleasant motor cruise
into the rough dusty drive the Alcan Highway was infamous
for.

Beautiful scenery and wide open tracts of land seemed
to impress the writers from more populous areas. An old cow
moose wandering out on the verge of the roadway helped to

provide the right setting for the trip.

Morale was high. Rumour suggested that Jimmy (Midnight) Anderson, the impressive bush pilot met by the press at the previous night's dinner, might attempt to land his Super Cub, 'Jackpine Savage' on the deck of one of the empty high-boy trailers being hauled south, for another payload of north-bound goods and equipment.

The outline of the freshly built 'wilderness lodge' greeted the tour as they arrived at Trutch Mountain, Mile 200, on the famous highway. The press viewed the log lodge and cabins, and then were to be flown into a fishing camp on the Besa River. Transportation would be Piper Super Cubs supplied by Jimmy Anderson and Ron Hanson. The two-seater aircraft normally could only carry one passenger. Short flying time and number of passengers deemed some modifications were necessary. This was achieved by first removing the back seat of the two-seated aircraft. A freight board made of half inch plywood was then installed forming a solid floor base behind the pilot's seat. The smallest of two passengers would then crawl back into the fuselage, and sit on a cross member support bar which was welded to the airplane sides. This left enough room for the larger of the pair to climb in front of the first, allowing the two-seated super cub to now carry three people on the short bush flight.

The Savage picked up speed. The tail end lifted and soon the aircraft lifted from Anderson's strip. The trained eye of the press observed the airstrip also seemed to serve as the main street of Trutch.

Seventeen minutes air time replaced the gruelling day's horseback ride to the Besa River fishing holes. The flight ended as Ron Hanson and Jimmy landed their cubs, on a hastily built flight strip used by oil companies some years earlier. The smoothness of the landing field was marred by overgrown buck brush (a local willow) and the occasional washout.

BESA RIVER CAMP

The day had been great as volunteer drivers, bank manager Doug Rolheiser, and Fort St. John Alderman Annette Pearson, led the scenic drive up the Alaska Highway. The group had been given a tour of a more than adequate base camp at Trutch Mountain. It had been a memorable flight to the fishing camp including a sighting of a moose herd. Cameraman Shig Fujita, of Asahi Evening News, Tokyo, sitting in the centre seat of the Jackpine Savage, achieved eye level shots of a cow moose and calf, browsing on the tender buds among the brush as the aircraft made a low silent pass over the muskeg.

Beef, veal or pork steaks cooked on sticks for that 'wilderness flavour' headed up the dinner menu. The barbecue was finished with a 'wee dram,' and a singsong around the campfire led by guitarists Herb and Judy Leake ended the day with everyone in good spirits. Reviews for northern B.C. travel industry were bound to be good!!

The Besa River campsite was designed for roughing it. Fortunately the weather was warm and the moon illuminated the wide sky country. When new bedrolls and ground sheets were handed out, some elected to sleep under the stars rather than in the small tents provided. A little mosquito repellent and the camp had settled for the night. Then, from deep in the darkened northern sky, came a distant drone of the now familiar Jackpine Savage.

Within minutes the super cub dropped out of the starlit sky. Landing lights scouring the bush strip, Midnight Anderson set down without a hitch. He had brought in some equipment for the next day's adventure. Unfortunately, there was no extra bedding. The only thing he had for warmth was a 26 ouncer which he and Horst spent most of the night nursing and discussing the next days trip.

A few of the outdoor writers were not completely in harmony with nature and rose a little stiff and sore from sleeping on the barren ground in the 3/4 length sleeping bags Horst had supplied. There was some murmuring about the grounds in the 'cowboy coffee' cooked over an open fire and the shortage of hot water in the wash basins. A tasty breakfast prepared by Judy and Herb Leake soon improved the atmosphere about the wilderness camp.

A two hour trail ride was arranged from the Besa up to an old Shell Oil drilling site. Herb and the Gillis boys had their hands full loading the Dude ponies with city riders, but soon had every thing under control. Pat Gillis led out the dude train for a scenic trek through the wilderness, giving the photographers in the group an excellent opportunity to get pictures of the fabulous "wilderness" scenery. His brother Paul took the rear of the twenty horse train to keep a eye on possible stragglers. Herb would stay behind and help his father-in-law Hersch Neighbour and Jimmy, build the wilderness rafts.

HERSCH

Whack! went the axe as the last branch disappeared from the long slender pole. Hersch looked critically at the slight nob left and using the axe blade as a chisel whisked the pole clean. Jimmy had pointed out the possibility of the inner tubes becoming ruptured by the constant rubbing of the wood protrusions.

Snap! went the rubber band cut from one of the inner

HERSCH NEIGHBOUR

tubes Jimmy had brought in on the last flight. Glancing towards the change in r.p.m. Hersch could see Jimmy point at the small compressor, say something to Horst and then started down the path from the flight strip to the river rolling a large inner tube before him. Dropping the tube on the beach next to where the rafts were being built Jimmy inspected a corner tie and said to Hersch "better put another band on this we don't want a break up going down the river."

Well that did it!

Hersch had been asked by his son-in-law to pilot one of the big Zodiac rafts that Horst Breithaupt was to supply for the trip. Two nights ago Jimmy had dropped in at the Alpine ranch and explained to Herb the seven layer rubber rafts had not arrived and the whole trip would have to be called off unless rafts could be made on site. Herb and his foster brother Paul Gillis had just finished the trip and although somewhat challenging in the small raft at the ranch, with a large raft and four to six people paddling, the trip would be a piece of cake. "Tell Horst we'll need about six paddles per craft," said Herb, "two dozen would cover it quite nicely."

The only paddle Hersch had seen so far was the one that Horst brought with him and the only damned thing he liked about these contraptions of Jimmy's is no matter what side landed up the thing would float.

Camp set, Hersch had started cutting spruce saplings out of the bush yesterday, he figured with the trail ride and raft trip all on the next day he had better get some poles gathered to build the rafts with. Starting at sunup. Hersch, his son-in-law and the Gillis boys, herded twenty two horses from the Alpine ranch to the Besa camp. The thirty mile ride and setting up camp Hersch was use to, but hauling the spruce poles from the bush had made it a long day. Wakened twice by the murmuring coming from the late night campfire,

Hersch's usual good nature was slightly ruffled this morning.

This had been the third time Jimmy had commented on the rubber wear attached to the raft. 'Jimmy' declared Hersch, 'I know your dad a while now and if he had been as concerned about rubber as you are, you wouldn't be here today!'

With that said the bush pilot smiled, pulled his hat down over his eyes and headed back towards the plane where the tube Horst had been sitting, was almost ready to remove from the vibrating compressor.

A flash of brown moving in the upstream brush indicated to Hersch the crew was on its way back. Horst from the elevated runway must have seen the train arriving also as he was rushing to the two horses that were tied to a tree half way up the trail towards the flight strip. Throwing the left stirrup over the saddle horn, Horst grabbed the cinch that had been loosened on the standing animal and with a jerk tightened the saddle to the dude `wise' pony. Hersch thought he should warn Horst to knee the stomach for bloat, but the self proclaimed woodsman seemed to ignore advice and was the loud one that sat up with Jimmy through the night, burning all the dry split firewood Hersch had ready for his daughter's breakfast fire. Whack! Another nob flew from slender pole Hersch was preparing as Horst thundered down the river trail to meet the dude train.

Horst Breithaupt pulled up in a small clearing as the first of the city cowboys pulled up. After a short meeting the man in charge turned the spirited mount and raced back to camp. At full gallop, the pony loosened cinch allowed the saddle to slip sideways and simulating a Charlie Chaplin movement, Horst was deposited head first into the northern shrubbery.

The excitement of the race and freedom of one of their

own gave the cagy ponies an occasion to act up and the exhibition made a turn for the worse when one of the spirited bush ponies decided to provide an early morning rodeo. Yono Yano, assistant editor of Junon Magazine of Tokyo, happened to be astride this little keg of dynamite as it went through its 'after ride' aerobics, throwing Yano over the shaggy-haired ears of his bronco. A couple of other writers found themselves unceremoniously dumped on the hard terrain before things got straightened out. Yono Yano was not hurt, but the fall was the start of a very unlucky day for the young assistant editor from Japan.

Learning saddle technique got more than a few jeers and just as many cuts and bruises to the body of Horst Breithaupt. To the weather beaten face of the halfway valley rancher, Hersch Neighbour, a smile.

WILDERNESS RAFTS

Bill Dyer, editor of the Alaska Highway News, Fort St. John, was surprised and knew the other members of the associated chambers executive were unaware that Horst Breithaupt, owner of Wilderness Lodge, had not received the big grey Zodiac rafts he was supposed to provide for the eighteen mile journey down the Besa and Prophet Rivers.

The layered rubber Zodiac boats were more desirable for the creature comforts, but there was a certain uniqueness and challenge to riding the 'Wilderness Rafts' that Jimmy and the crew had constructed from spruce saplings. The spruce frames of the rafts were held together with large rubber bands that were made by cutting inner tubes in parallel strips. Using 3/8 rope and more rubber bands the frames were then lashed to truck inner tubes, that were inflated with the small gas air compressor brought in on last night's flight. The raft was then covered with a black plastic sheet. The crafts appeared to be quite sturdy and had been used to float big game out of the deep northern woods.

The paddles were made by cutting a slot into the end of a spruce pole with a chain saw. A triangular piece of 1/2 inch plywood was then inserted and held in place by nails driven into the sides of the pole through the plywood with the tip of the metal embedding into the other shank of the soft spruce. The paddles were adequate devices for experienced rafters, but in the hands of beginners, wouldn't hold up as well as the rafts.

Fishing for the elusive Dolly Varden trout and Arctic grayling while waiting for the rafts to be completed, Bill Rice of Western Outdoor News of Los Angeles, and Ken Castle of Outdoor Outlook of San Leandro, California demonstrated their expertise at the mouth of a clear stream flowing into the Besa river.

THE TRIP

On June 5, 1975 at 1:30 p.m. the expedition was ready to sail for a leisurely eighteen mile ride down the Besa. The twenty three rafters would be aboard four craft. The first would be captained by Herb Leake operator of the Alpine Ranch. Lennie Schubert would be helmsman on the second raft. Instead of one of the Gillis boys, Horst Breithaupt, owner of the Wilderness Lodge and expedition leader, insisted he run the raft containing two European writers, Horst's friend the financial comptroller, and at the last moment Pat Crofton. Hersch Neighbour would pilot the fourth. On the third raft, strapped to the spruce frame work was the lunch Horst was commissioned to supply.

The rafters would have lunch on the Prophet, and supper at the Alpine Ranch situated at the base of the northwest side of Pink Mountain. Jimmy, who was riding shotgun over the river operation, would fly, Judy Leake and Noella Desjardins of LaPresse, Montreal, down river in plenty of time to help Judy's sister Sandy Anderson (who was looking after her two nieces) prepare a large hot meal for the river crew. After dinner a short flight back to Trutch for an overnight stay at Horst's newly assembled Wilderness Lodge.

Although the river trip had been deemed safe, some of the people on the executive of the associated chambers had misgivings about the rafting expedition and had suggested to Bill Dyer that he call it off if things looked dangerous. The flat boats looked dependable and were rumoured to be seaworthy. The day was warm, and the calm sparkling waters of the Besa river invited all for a fun day of travel and excitement. There was going to be plenty of both.

River Ride

The calm and inviting sparkles of the river all too soon became a series of small and large rapids. The truck tube rafts bobbed like spruce cones on a clear mountain stream. The black plastic covering kept the river water from lapping up at the bottom side of the rafters. However, the larger rapids crashed over the primitive vessel, and segments of the Besa collected in pockets, as the plastic dipped into the centre of the tubes. The wild, cold river waters were captured, and momentarily prevented from returning to the northern tributary.

The first to be initiated by this constant change of cold water was Alaska Al. On June 1st, Al Kuchta had become the winner (by panning the nugget in seven seconds flat) of the World Invitational Class A Gold Panning Championship, held in Taylor, Mile 36 on the Alaska Highway. Al and his partner, Prospector John had dropped in at the Wilderness Lodge on the way back to Alaska and had been invited along to add a little colour to the trip. Seeing as how the two men had nothing pressing, it was decided to tag along with panning gear and check the Besa and Prophet for a little 'colour.'

The water had been sloshing over the two prospectors when Al spotted the extra inner tubes. He grabbed the tubes and went to the back of the wilderness built boat. Despite warnings by raft operator, Lennie Schubert, Al by stacking the tubes prepared himself a high very comfortable seat. In the first turbulent water, however, this springy recliner launched Alaska Al into the icy waters of the Besa River. A fisherman, when not prospecting, he swam strongly after the raft, and was able to climb back on by grabbing onto the pole paddle held out by others.

This proved to be one of the few things the paddles were good for as first one and then another was lost or broken as the inexperienced rafters were swept towards shore and of course the deadly sweepers. Built for paddling but not for poling, the spruce saplings when, used to fend off disaster, would stick and the polers were faced with giving up the paddles, or staying with their poles stuck either in the muddy bank or entangled in the maze of branches protruding from a sweeper.

A sweeper is a tree that has fallen from the bank and lies sleepily in the fast flowing river, with branches waiting just inches below the deceptive water to snag the unwary rafter. Once caught up on the downstream side, the current would push the upstream side of a vessel under water, flipping craft and riders into the rushing water.

Three minutes after the third raft departed, the self assured German financial expert decided to stab slots through the black plastic where the puddles had accumulated. The Puma White Hunter knife went through the plastic and into the inert floatation below creating a blowout in the foremost inner tube and a loss of buoyancy. This combined with the extra weight of the food made the Breithaupt raft difficult to steer. Horst, however, did not panic. This trip was designed so a little old lady could enjoy it. Captain Breithaupt, store bought oar beside him, stretched out on the raft to catch a few rays of the early afternoon sun. The crew of five floated down the Besa tributary into the Prophet River.

Run off from the melting snow caps had swollen the northern tributary and when emptying into the Prophet, it became a torrent of rapids swirling against the curving banks of the larger river. Whitewater, strengthened by two weeks of unseasonable warm weather as well as inexperience, prevented reasonable steering of the damaged craft. The shore came rushing at the third raft to leave the Besa camp and it was evident the vessel was not going to make the turn.

Violently thrown into the bank, the knife maimed raft operated by Horst Breithaupt was the first craft to flip over. Two of the group were thrown safely onto the shore. One was trapped under the raft held steadfast against the bank debris by the rushing current. Fortunately the two writers from Germany and Belgium tossed on the bank were able to save the German financial expert and salvage the damaged raft. Horst Breithaupt was thrown into the river, but being a strong swimmer was able to reach river edge. The overturned vessel carried all the food for the expedition. Fish were the only ones to lunch on the Prophet that afternoon.

Pat Crofton, the fifth member of the Breithaupt raft was thrown into the middle of the river and swept downstream. Bumping his knees and legs on slippery rocks the sixty year old gentleman from London, England, tried in vain to get a footing while he fought the force of the flow that kept bowling him over. Eventually Pat, shivering with muscles bruised, came to a gentle bend where the Prophet was more shallow. Grasping a boulder on the rocky bank Pat dragged himself out of the frigid waters. The pulled muscle in his left leg making movement very painful.

The area was heavily wooded. Pat knew that he had to find a place where he could be spotted from the other bank or the air. Moving down river he stumbled out of the mosquito infested bush onto a small sand bar. Pat was bitterly cold from the fifteen or twenty minutes he had been fighting the icy water of the glacier fed river. He felt the split lip, and noticed the cut on his hand, then realized the aged wedding band was missing from his finger.

"There is `gold' in the Prophet River," Pat wryly cracked a self indulgent joke as he clambered down the narrow bar seeking warmth from the sun.

Eventually the Jackpine Savage flew over. Alternately moving the joystick from left to right 'Midnight' made a waving motion with the wings indicating that he had seen Pat stranded on the sunny sanctuary.

All warmth dissipated by the cold exposure and wishing for a waxed match to light a fire using the dry driftwood lying in abundance on the small bar, Pat waited.

LUNCH

The three remaining rafts were beached together on a large gravel bar just after the tour reached the Prophet River. The constant spray of icy waters demanded a large driftwood fire be built to dry out `behinds' and warm chilly bones.

Crashing through waves three and four feet high, the panicky oarsmen had snapped the fragile plywood inserts of the bush made paddles fending off the rocky shores. Poles were cut from the bush to replace the broken paddles that had been lost. The primitive vessels now had to be steered by poling fore and aft. Although at a disadvantage without the steering capabilities of the paddles, the solidly built crafts could be directed downstream in a fair fashion.

It was while waiting safe and dry on the designated beach where lunch was to be served that the three rafting crews learned of the ill fate of the Breithaupt vessel. First having the blowout, and then thrown into the river bank causing lunch to be postponed. Horst and crew were alright, but at that time stranded up river and were presently using the sabotaged raft to float to a point where the super cub could pick them up and ferry them to the ranch.

This was relayed to the rafters by Jimmy Anderson, who had been monitoring the episode from the air. Swooping down onto the gravel bar, he demonstrated the ability of the Jackpine Savage III to land and take-off in unbelievable short distances. This feat would prove to be more than useful.

Some of the Japanese rafters made it known they wanted to fly out with Jimmy, and to heck with the rest of the river trip. Jimmy indicated that the landing area was too short to take off with extra weight and advised everyone to persevere. There just was not any trouble between where the rafts had landed and the ranch. Reassured, the apprehensive rafters re-embarked for the lazy afternoon drifting down the river to the ranch, and the hot meal that would be awaiting them.

Some of the river rats became so confident of the smooth waters bearing their craft along, they removed their life jackets. These lifesavers would now be used as padding to protect their delicate posteriors from the annoying protrusions of those spruce saplings. Things were good. Morale was once again high.

The Schubert vessel carrying the Japanese writer, Yono

Yano, and cameraman, J. Oishi, Bill Dyer, Alaska Al, and Prospector John were doing fairly well and a good part of the distance had been covered. The rafters were becoming quite confident of their ability to handle the sturdy craft with the poles.

Then without warning, the treacherous current swept the raft towards the bank, as it had done countless times before that day. However, this time it encountered a root sweeper, unlike the old sweepers they had been constantly avoiding which had fallen from the forest into the river. This tree had fallen back into the timber, leaving the Prophet waters to eat deep into the root-infested gravel bank. Faster than a muskrat sliding down a mud bank, the creative current sucked the Schubert raft into the huge protruding root structure, that once held the timeless timber in the air. The raft momentarily was steadfast against the root structure, then the current rushed over the upstream side of the raft pushing that side under water and flipping the whole raft.

Bill Dyer was to have a first hand view of the disaster.

RIVER RESCUE

A movement in the timber, Crofton glued his eyes to the spot. Another flash of white as Pat saw an animal pass by the small opening in the treed cover. Soon Paul Gillis riding "Joker" a large white gelding appeared on the opposite bank of the Prophet. Deadheading the horses packed with tents and gear from the Besa camp back to the ranch with his brother Pat, the pair had been kept busy rounding up the Breithaupt crew and shepherding them to a place of rescue by the Jackpine savage. Leaving Pat with the herd, Paul forded the river with two horses.

Joker in the lead, with the pony Pat was astride being led by Paul, the horses waded into the murky waters of the

Prophet. Pat felt the footing of his steed occasionally break away from the river bottom and then touch again as the two ponies strived to keep their footing. Looking over to Paul with worn desperation in his voice Pat said. "I don't think I can survive another dunking, are we going to make it across?" Paul in a reassuring tone that covered his own concerns said. "Just close your eyes and hang onto the saddle horn and I'll get us across." Pat knew immediately he was not going to close his eyes, but took the advice of the guide and tightened the death grip he already had on the leather covered saddle horn.

Once across the river Paul led the fifth member of the Breithaupt crew back upstream, to a spot where the seasoned guide figured a plane could land. This turned out to be a short space along side the river, very rocky with a stand of trees hovering over the native landing strip.

Pat watched as Jimmy Anderson, with great skill, landed his plane with only feet to spare. The bush pilot and his plane were a most welcome sight for Pat.

The Super Cub strived for height as it lifted off the scant stony runway. Completely exhausted Pat Crofton momentarily closed his eyes. It appeared take off altitude would not be sufficient to clear the scrub spruce directly in front of the aircraft. The fatigued Director of Tourism reluctantly watched as the tips of the aged spruce seemed to touch the oversized tandem bush tires as they passed over the ancient vegetation. Heading towards the Alpine ranch, Pat relaxed and smiled, for this rescue flight, he thought, "I will be forever grateful to `Jimmy Anderson,' and the `Jackpine Savage.'"

SUBMARINE CREW
Glacier fed streams rush down the mountains into the

fast moving Besa tributary. The Besa then flows into the
Prophet river. On a sunny day in June there is nothing like a
wake-up call from Mother Nature given by a sudden dunking
in those frigid northern waters.

Bill Dyer, Editor, of Alaska Highway News was
swimming well below the surface and thinking that it was a
good thing he had his life jacket on as he did not swim very
well. Then Bill remembered that he had used his life jacket to
sit on, it was probably thrown into the river like everything
else on the raft. Bill tried to recall those Red Cross
commercials telling one to take slow, easy strokes and above
all not to panic in situations like this. It worked! He got to the
surface and found his life jacket floating right next to him and
the raft not far away. Fighting for air and continuation, Bill
grabbed the jacket with one hand and flailed his way towards
the lifesaving vessel. His water-filled cowboy boots dragged
by the undertow towards the shadowy roots emerging from
the icy water.

Bill Dyer had donned western garb to add local flavour
to the trip, but found that cowboy boots were not the
recommended gear for swimming in the Prophet River. The
Fort St. John newspaper editor would have gladly traded his
weighted boots for the tennis shoes of that little old lady, who
this trip was designed for.

Achieving the raft and cheating the river, Bill noted that
J. Oishi, the Japanese cameraman and Lennie Schubert had
also managed to grab on. Bobbing up and down the second
rafter from Japan was hanging on to a small log protruding
from the angry current. Yono Yano hung on for dear life.
Lennie pulled the raft towards shore and now was above his
knees in rushing water about fourteen feet down stream from
the Japanese writer, yelling to let go. Lennie finally convinced
Yono to give in to the dragging current and relaxed his frozen

grip on the life saving log. The river immediately carried Yono to the waiting grasp of Captain Schubert who was being slowly dragged down stream by the current driven raft.

Everyone hung on, and gradually worked their way to the rocky shore on the other side of the river, leaving the two prospectors from Alaska safe but stranded, on the opposite bank of the Prophet. The prospectors had been able to clamber out of the cold water minus their gear and hats. Although left high and dry on the side of the river, they now faced the dilemma of reuniting with the rest of the crew and raft.

When the shore was reached, Bill Dyer realized they didn't have matches, an axe or anything except the raft and the clothes on their backs. Even Bill's black cowboy hat along with the hats of John and Al had gone floating down the Prophet. Morale was dampening.

Anderson swooped low to check that everyone was alright. He had come by on the way back upstream to where the crew of the disabled Breithaupt raft, containing the blown tube, was again in trouble. This time a small sweeper had upset the raft.

The crew on the third raft piloted by Hersch Neighbour stopped and built a fire so the partial crew of dampened river rats from the Schubert vessel could get warm and somewhat dry. Hersch cut some poles to replace the ones lost in the capsizing. Twice now he had used the wooden matches contained in his metal water proof container. Riding tail end on this rafting trip was starting to become quite a job.

Hersch had started out behind the Breithaupt raft but unlike Horst whom elected to float the river current, Hersch directed his crew to paddle to the middle and ride the crest of the waves. Keeping the raft in the centre of the river and away from the shore and sweepers would be the ticket for this ride.

WINGS ON THE PROPHET

In disbelief Hersch swept pass Horst and his disarranged crew. Hersch did not know how long Breithaupt was staying in the north, but if Horst wanted to leave alive, he had better gain a bit more respect for the woods.

The distraught Schubert river crew was assured once again from the air by Anderson who, by cutting the engine, glided through the clear air and swooped in low over the gravel bar like a large bird fishing the river. Sliding the side cockpit window open, Jimmy shouted, 'stay in the middle, everything O.K.' There were no more problem areas from their dunking spot to the ranch and a warm, country style, home cooked meal.

Grudgingly Yono took the wet life jacket from Hersch Neighbour and slipped the heavy garment over his shoulders, then climbing aboard, the rafters continued on the ill-fated journey watching for a spot on the other side of the river where they could beach and rescue the prospectors. Alaska Al and John had to walk a mile along the steep rock and brush-covered shore before reaching the small gravel bar stretching into the river. Al had lost one boot in the upset and found the going difficult. Although discouraged with rafting, Al and John both agreed it beat the hell out of walking along the intractable shores of the Prophet river.

A grimace came to Hersch's face as his own flirt with destiny became obvious. The shortage of life jackets dictated that Hersch travel without that cumbersome lifesaver being strapped to him. The sturdy Austrian writer, travelling on Hersch's raft, reached to cut another piece of the 3/8 inch rope Hersch had tied to the raft which was used to tie the paddles securely in a primitive oar lock. Pieces had been cut a few times before from this twenty feet of rope trailing from the aft. Constant use had worn out several ropes and all the extra rubber bands.

When questioned why he insisted on leaving a dozen feet of rope attached, Hersch was forced to confess to the crew. The line stretched out behind the raft would be used as a lifeline if the raft ever tipped. Hersch confided, although he had swam many a horse across rivers, spring flood or not and had forded many streams with a pack on his back. Recreation in the cold northern rivers was seldom thought of and Hersch Neighbour had just never leaned to swim.

Rosemary, a writer from the Victoria Travel, willingly surrendered a fine leather belt from her jacket. The Austrian writer immediately attached the leather strap to his oar lock and in a vibrant voice sang praises to the woman he called "Rose Marie."

On went the Schubert vessel carrying Lennie, Bill Dyer, the Alaska prospectors and Japanese newsmen. All were down in the mouth, dampened, Huckleberry Finns. Meagre was the enthusiasm for fending off the rocky shores with the fresh cut poles. Morale fell to even greater depths when the second sweeper hit.

Every man jack was wearing his life jacket. River experience had trained the crew, who grabbed the raft on the way over.

Everyone climbed back aboard the upside down raft and drifted along until it came to a log jam that jutted into the powerful current of the Prophet River.

Skipper Lennie Schubert grabbed one of the logs sticking out from the jam. Fearful of getting sucked underneath by the powerful undertow, everyone scrambled off the raft onto the logs and safety of the bank, leaving the unmanned ship to be broke up by the swelling current and hurled aimlessly downstream by the merciless rapids.

Shortly after, with crew paddling intensely, the Neighbour vessel cruised past the log jam and beached river rats. Hirsh noted that every one was safe on the bank. Two rafts were now destroyed and without a gravel bar to pull over to, Hersch could be of no more help to the Schubert crew. They would have to count on Jimmy to airlift them to his daughter's supper table.

Relayed through the air Jimmy had told Hersch that Herb and crew were safely rafting quite some distance down stream. With no one left to look out for, Hersch would now finish this river journey and get some warm food into the stomachs of his crew of five.

Engine drone was heard as the Schubert river survivors strained to see Anderson's super cub, Jackpine Savage III. The party was hidden by the growth along the bank, and were unable to make contact with the man who was riding shotgun on this truly 'wilderness experience.'

A person just doesn't appreciate how cold it can be on a sunny afternoon along the Prophet until they have been thoroughly soaked in icy water a couple of times and then dumped solemnly on the shady side of the big spruce that grew on the banks of the snow fed waterway. Hypothermia ate away at the hungry bodies of the battered river crew.

After walking downstream along the bank, the chilled crew had to climb across a nature built bridge made of river fallen trees, stretching out over the swift-moving stream, to a large open gravel bar on the end of a Prophet River island. Soaking wet and numbed from immersion in the water, the Schubert rafters tried jogging and swinging their arms to warm up and prayed for the plane to come over and at least drop a box of matches.

It wasn't long until Anderson winged over, air lifting to safety one of the Breithaupt crew who had dumped twice also. Jimmy shortly returned and after checking the situation carefully from the air, put his plane down on the rocky shore. Some time was spent 'building an airstrip.' By clearing the larger rocks to form a long narrow runway, the aircraft could take off with the extra weight of a passenger. The Schubert crew was then warmed at a fire made by Jimmy, and eventually the whole group was airlifted off the small island, one at a time.

Alderman Annette Pearson grabbed the spruce railing of the raft as once again the craft piloted by Herb Leake was hurled towards the rocky shore by the angry water. The northern raised Alderman could see first hand the dangers of the two weeks of warm weather rising the water level of the river. The meandering water way changed to a water torrent dividing and joining forces, pushing past banks sometimes three miles wide, and eventually emptying into the Muskwa River.

The raft hit the shore hard. Castle, the tall American writer, grabbed Shig Fujita, just as the writer from Japan was going over the side. On the next bend the group was hit by a protruding tree trunk. It's earth barren roots reaching into the river from the shore swept Bill Rice, from Los Angeles, over board. Wide eyed and her heart beating wildly with excitement, Alderman Pearson held out her rafting pole to the American reporter. The other rafters pulled the river soaked western outdoor news writer from the icy waters.

Widening of the banks slowed the river and broke it once again into several narrow slow moving channels. Quietness of the river caused Annette to relax. Thankful her craft had the experience of Herb Leake and the strength of the outdoor writers, to keep their raft mid stream and out of danger, she drifted off. Remembering the good natured joking about the fate of the now safe Breithaupt vessel and it's submarine crew, brought a smile to her sun warmed face. Annette remembered the big fire on the gravel bar where lunch was to have been served and wished that heat was available now. Drifting down the river with distant Humming noises of the Jackpine Savage,(ferrying yet more members of the submarine crews to the safety of the ranch), lulled the tired girl into momentarily closing her eyes. The whole trip had been quite an experience.

Landing at the flight strip yesterday afternoon was delayed as Jimmy had to buzz the ponies three times to shoo the twenty some head away from the lush grass growing wild on the runway.

Wind flowing through her hair Annette raced Herb's horse along the beach. One of the few riders on the trip that knew horses she had drawn the high spirited lead horse. Running the animal didn't seem to slow this pony. On the trail Annette had constant problems with the horse trying to pass the pony in front of him. Ambition drove Herb's lead horse as he cut through the bush to a switch back in the trail that put the competitive horse in the lead and an end to Annette's first real bush ride.

Leading on the way back Annette was not impressed as Horst came roaring up to the small clearing to speak with the German man He had been hovering around. She was even less impressed when Horst wheeled around and raced back to camp. Pedigree in her northern horse was not dampened by the thirty mile trek it had made yesterday from the Alpine Ranch to Besa camp and in a moment leaped to the challenge of Horst's running mount. Moments away from another race through the woods Annette quickly pulled Herb's horse back under control. Others in the group, including Horst's financial friend from Germany were not as lucky. Rewarding was the sight as each leap Horst's galloping animal took, the mounted rider with saddle, dropped a few more degrees towards the ground.

RIVER ATTACK

Sudden excitement rippling through the seasoned crew drew Annette's attention downstream. A calf and cow

RIVER ATTACK

moose had scrambled down the bank of the narrow channel into the river and was swimming across, intercepting the rafts course. Slowly the floating craft drifted towards the swimming pair.

Ken Castle of Outdoor Outlook squatted atop the

WALKING OUT

vessel prepared to take a picture of the animals, once their
hoofs touched river bottom not 30 feet away. At that time,

Herb Leake, sensing trouble, jumped into the knee deep water
to push the raft towards shore to keep from colliding with the
pair. Under Herb's direction, once stopped, the crew would
jump ship for the more solid footing of the rocky bank. The
jolt of the raft suddenly stopping as it bumped against the
coarse river bottom was enough to dump the intrigued camera
man into the river, not far from a slightly irritated female
moose who felt her calf was in danger.

Instinctively, the motherley northern moose headed in
the direction of the southern California writer and make shift
vessel. San Leandro California, seemed like a long ways away
as Ken Castle scrambled for the safety of river edge.

Missing Castle in her charge the irate mother went
wild. Neck and back hair on end, with ears flat back the moose
stood on her back legs and to Annette's amazement
proceeded to stomp on the beached raft, snapping the fragile
poles. Leaving broken parts of the craft to continue on down
the Prophet River.

Drenched each time the rapids leaped over the plastic
coverings, Annette had been cold sitting on top the wind
swept rafts. She was not overly bothered by the fact that it laid
on the banks of the Prophet in pieces. Vandalized by the
disappearing bulk of the wilderness beast indignantly trotting,
with her offspring in tow, out of sight.

WALKING OUT

No lunch, and a six hour river trip, made for a very
tired Fort St. John Alderperson who climbed up the gravel
bank of the Prophet River, just as the sun dipped behind the
Rocky Mountain giants. Annette's discovery of gas lamps,
shining from the Leake's ranch house window across the
darkening alpine, quickened her pace. Wet and cold, Annette
realized a half an hour walk would put her near a warm fire

and hot supper in Herb and Judy's log home.

Gamely trudging along side, Shig Fujita the Japanese writer, was muttering about the 'wilderness adventure,' turning out to be more of a 'wilderness survival course!'
Flying Out

The Japanese writers from the demised Schubert vessel insisted that this time they were not only flying off the river, they wanted to be the first of the Schubert crew to be flown to the Alpine Ranch. Inside the belly of the aircraft, Yono, assistant editor of Junon magazine of Tokyo, knew this was the right decision. Getting on to this gravel bar by risking his life crossing over swiftly moving water using a narrow nature fallen bridge was not Yono's idea of a great time. Already to day he had been thrown from a half wild bush pony. Then coaxed onto a raft, floated down an isolated river in the middle of nowhere and flipped not once but twice into the icy, clammy waters of Northeastern B.C.

Now at last he was off of that dreadful raft. Yono looked forward to a nice dry plane ride to safety.

The Jackpine Savage III taxied down the makeshift runway. Yono watched the banks of the Prophet race by, as the super cub picked up take-off speed along the rough gravel bar. Looking up over the pilot's shoulder, he could see the huge stump coming up on the left of the aircraft.

The budding assistant editor from Japan remembered questioning Jimmy about the immovable object as they fashioned a crude flight strip out of the wilderness shore. The bush pilot assured the young editor the Savage would have enough altitude to clear the stump.

Twice already today Yono had been assured that things were going to be alright and twice he had been disappointed. That damn stump was coming towards them, at over sixty kilometres per hour. He could see the wing strut was not going to be high enough to miss the jagged protrusion. It was a very disillusioned young passenger from Japan, who braced himself for the impact that would rip the wing from the body of the aircraft. Scattering passengers and parts of the Jackpine Savage III, all over the banks of the Prophet River.

With only moments to impact, the pilot, whose flying skill had already impressed youthful Yono, banked the plane slightly and the wing strut skimmed over the large stump.

Greatly relieved, Yono glanced from the wing to the nose of the plane and immediately realized the slight bank had turned the Jackpine Savage towards a large spruce hanging over the river, the rushing current eating away at its decaying root structure.

At an elevation of sixty feet, the Savage was thrown into a hard left bank. 'G' forces pushed Yono hard into his seat. Wings tipped vertical to the earth, the big spruce passed beneath the aircraft. The flight path levelled out and Yono felt the muscles of his river-torn body relax when the nose of the Savage headed in the direction of the single luminescence of light in the whole valley and warm, dry clothing with a hot supper prepared by Judy Leake at the Alpine ranch.

Bill Dyer was the last member of the six man Schubert crew to be air lifted off. Bill being the largest of the crew members waiting for their turn, had made sure the flight strip was as smooth and as long as possible.

The super cub laboured for altitude as the wing strut cleared the old stump, the Savage at once went into a hard port bank to miss the deadly old growth. The editor of Alaska Highway News remembered a comment from one of his committee members, wondering if Jimmy had got his allegedly revoked flying licence, back from the Department of Transport. Regardless, he would not have traded even one of his river-worn, water-soaked cowboy boots for a pilot, other than Jimmy Midnight Anderson to lift him out of this predicament.

He decided this was not the time to ask the veteran pilot if he was licensed for this kind of flying!

Carrying two women from the B.C. Government, the vessel piloted by Hersch Neighbour was the only one of the four to complete the 'Wilderness Experience' by water. The river expertise of the 68 year old grandfather of thirteen guided the raft safely down stream, but did not arrive at his daughters ranch and a hot meal until 10 p.m. that night. All were fed, and ferried back through the darkened northern star lit night sky to the Wilderness Lodge in a three passenger Cessna, and Jimmy's Super Cub 'The Jackpine Savage.'

Friday July 4, 1975 Shig Fujita reported to the English language Asaki Evening News wrote:

"Of the 23 persons who took the river trip 11 got dumped twice, and two others once each. Six cameras became water logged and no longer usable. I can understand that those who planned the trip had the very best of intentions, and wanted to give us as interesting an experience as possible. However, they seemed to get carried away by their enthusiasm, and forgot to take the comfort and safety of the participants into adequate consideration.

The rafts, in the first place, were unmanageable and unsafe. The distance of 18 kilometres was much too long, three or four kilometres would have been adequate to give us an idea of what was available. When I relate our experience of the raft ride, people laugh and seem to find our adventure amusing, but I can assure you that at the time we were miserably cold, frankly worried and not a little frightened. Of course, I cannot deny it was a most unusual experience."

PROSPECTING THE AKIE

*O*n a crisp September afternoon, Matriarch, a moose grandmother 12 years old and starting to show her age, led the little herd of six, for which she was responsible, down a soft, leafy trail onto a rocky bar jutting into the Akie River. Lifting her nose high to sniff the clear, chilly air and signalling the others to follow, she entered into the grove of willow shrubs and alder that lined the river banks. The grandmother may have heard the reverberating sounds of an aircraft engine breaking the northern silence. If she did she ignored it, and the pace she set was in anticipation of the feast that she was leading her small band to.

She had in her herd two daughters, each of whom had two offspring, heifer and bull to the elder, bull and heifer to the younger. In obedience to the instincts of her race, and to the specific impulses which stemmed from her being female, she devoted her entire life to her herd, especially the young. If in her constant foraging she caught even a hint that her four grandchildren were not getting their share, she would forego her own feeding to see to it that they ate first. This characteristic, which separated her from other moose grandmothers, had developed because of her monomania affection for her offspring.

This same characteristic now moved her and her family further away from the small gravel bar to the feast awaiting. Had Matriarch and her grandchildren stopped to browse on the drying grass and willow tips, they would have seen the super cub and heard the R.P.M. cut of the 150 H.P. Lycoming engine as the aircraft touched the tandem oversized bush tires onto the sloping banks of the Akie River.

GOING IN

From the back seat, prospector Jack saw the all-too-short gravel bar speed by his side window as the cub once again set down on the rough strip. Then again the throttle was pushed forward and the Jackpine Savage lifted back into the air.

"We're going to try'er buds," Jack nodded affirmative to the pilot Jimmy Anderson, who had pointed out the huge tree that had fallen from the bank across the tip of the bar and partly into the river.

"With the head winds the way they are, we can set down, brake with the bush tires and stop before we hit that boulder," Jim explained referring to a large rock that had rolled from the side of the cliff that was bordering the Akie River. Jack knew the situation. Once landed, he and Jim would roll the huge boulder out into the river, and with the two axes they had in the back end of the Jackpine Savage, the old sweeper at the beginning of the bar would be history. Jack realized the first landing would be hazardous but the prospector had a feeling about this area and fully realized the risks in the prospecting game that he loved. The second landing, when supplies were brought in, would be a piece of cake.

The aircraft was nosed into the air current and down towards the gravel bar. The purpose of the flight had been to look over the terrain, but the Savage had been loaded light just in case the upstream gust was strong enough to land on the edge of the Akie. Jimmy had seen the cloud formation in the far distance. Cold weather was moving in. The landing had to be made today because of the short braking distance. Snow or even frost on the rocks would make the initial landing impossible. The aircraft swooped in low over the grey, brittle branches of the discarded tree. The joy-stick of the Savage was eased back and the drag flaps snapped into place as the bush tires once again touched and settled down on the gravel bar. Then one of those things that happen while landing on mountain rivers happened. The wind quit!!

The pilot realized that without the head wind he would not be able to brake the speed of the aircraft before the fragile under-carriage was ripped from the Jackpine Savage's belly. In an instant he slammed the throttle forward and threw the flaps off. The Lycoming motor roared back to life as the joy-stick demanded enough height for the airplane's landing gear to just clear the rock. Without the help of nature's wind however, the invention of man hung in the air above the river, as the labouring prop tried to pull the dead weight of the Savage back into the clear blue sky.

Jimmy saw right away , the dilemma. If the aircraft wings did manage to find an up-draft in the next second or so, he might get enough lift to slam him and the Savage into the high cliffs bordering the Akie as the river rounded a bend. The other option was to bank to the starboard side as he had in the previous passes at the impending strip, then circle out over the scrub-spruce that covered the lower bank of the tributary. But, to turn the Savage at stall speed would only allow the aircraft to slide wing tip first into the solid spruce timber. The veteran pilot had one option—"put'er down in the Akie." Quick as a bush pilot trying to save his livelihood, Jimmy killed the Lycoming and nosed the Jackpine Savage II once again towards the Akie River.

Prospector Jack had concerns when the super cub had almost collided with the boulder. He had flown with Jim before and had no doubt that he was the best for this kind of bush flying. However, he was now gliding through the air to what looked like a river landing. Jack was used to taking high risks in the prospecting business, but this was getting a little out of control!!

The resistant head wind was flowing upstream, so the

opposing airship was gliding in the same direction as the river current. The water landing was surprisingly smooth and the Savage turned from aircraft to watercraft. The new-found relief was soon disrupted by another boulder that had fallen from the high river banks and submerged itself in the crystal clear water. The bush tires of the aquaplane brushed up

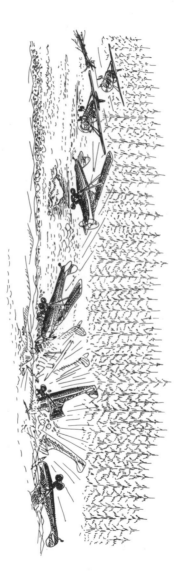

against the large rock halting the floating craft momentarily. The Savage had stopped, but the Akie had not. The current built up under the fuselage, lifting the tail of the craft high into the air and shoving the now still motor underwater. The plane somersaulted end for end, freeing the jammed bush tires which ended up, perched on top of the Jackpine Savage which was floating like a large bird of prey. Wings outstretched. Belly-up! Dead in the water!!

The upside-down occupants of the Savage fought to get their seat belts undone as visions of the craft going down into the icy waters were very real. Pilot and passenger squirmed out the opened side door and crawled onto the wing, immediately realizing that the air in the wings of the aircraft shell was keeping the Savage afloat. They slipped into the icy waters and by kicking their feet they could direct the vessel as the current accelerated it towards the bank boasting a thick covering of the rugged spruce. Half a mile downstream from the original landing site, the Savage once again touched the rocky banks of the Akie as it was pushed up onto the gravel bar by the river-chilled men.

SURVIVING

Prospector Jack was disturbed by Jimmy's behaviour. Jimmy had spent most of the afternoon just sitting on the river bank looking at the remains of the Savage. Occasionally he would walk down to the plane. Starting at the tail section that was resting on the edge of the river bank he would enter the icy waters, then walk around the outstretched wings which other than being filled with two feet of water, did not look damaged. When he reached the long prop attached to the front of the Lycoming motor the water was at waist level. With a root shovel he prodded the gravel and sand bottom of the Akie. Jack watched as the concerned pilot came back, slipping on the fresh

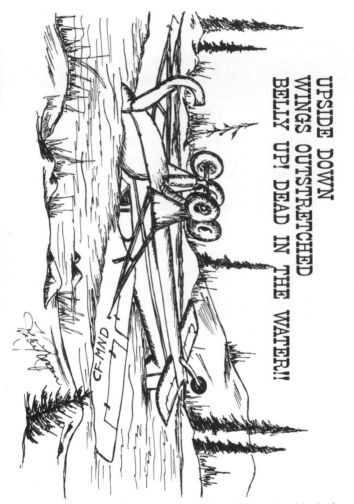

frost that lay heavily on the rocky shore. Sliding into his denim
jeans that were warming on the rocks, Jimmy stoked the fire that

was always going to keep away the cold bite of the Akie River.

Jack thought back to yesterday evening when he and Jim had dragged themselves up onto the gravel bar that was to be their home for the next seven days. They had immediately started a fire with the abundant driftwood that was left high and dry by countless spring run-off. Wet clothing was shed with jerking movements as hypothermia probed deep into the muscles of both men. The warmth of the blaze gradually penetrated the cold and soon movement became less rigid.

Heading back to the downed aircraft, the two men, now warm, once again entered the water. This time it was to empty the fuselage. The contents consisted of two axes, an air pump to assure proper tire pressure for various terrain landings, one-half dozen plastic vomit bags tucked in the map pocket attached to the back of the pilot seat (just for the occasional passenger that found the various landings stomach wrenching), an eight-inch crescent wrench, a six-inch flat head screwdriver, a pair of pliers, two aircraft seats, one hundred feet of 3/8 inch rope, a quart of oil and a piece of 1/2 inch plywood three feet long, two feet wide at one end, and eighteen inches wide at the other. This was removed from behind the passenger seat where it was used as solid base when putting freight in the fragile tin holding area. Survival food consisted of a pound of ground coffee and a can of spaghetti and meatballs. Any food other than this would have to be acquired with the survival gear that always travelled with the Savage when flying in the   north.

A brown leather holster filled with a Smith and Wesson 45 calibre semi-automatic was stashed under the pilot's seat along with a bone-handled knife. The knife in its sheath was attached to a hand-tooled pistol belt, which sported a neat row of 45 calibre cartridges. Jack had brought along his 357 Magnum firearm with the 9-inch barrel that he fondly referred to as his bear gun and, naturally, had a large hunting knife and adequate ammo attached to the gun belt.

The aroma of spaghetti and meatballs drifted along the remote gravel bar as darkness slowly began to fall. Jack held the knife-opened lid with pliers as he gingerly stirred the contents of the tin with a freshly-cut twig. He did not want to burn any of this precious meal. The hot banquet was going to sit well in the chilled stomachs of the stranded men. Unknown to Jack this would be their last food for four days other than the coffee that would be boiled in the same tin as the meal now being cooked.

First thing this morning , as frost hung in the cold mountain air. Jim and Jack with axes in hand ,had wandered back into the thick forest looking for dead or semi-dead spruce, about three to four inches in diameter. When a suitable tree was found the root base was exposed and earth removed as low as possible so the valuable tools did not lose their sharp edge on the dulling dirt. A file, at this time, was not carried on the downed Savage.

The root and about five feet of two fallen trees were brought to the campsite. The fibrous root was soaked in the river to remove the remaining dirt and soften the aged spruce tuber. Jim took the washed pole to a fallen log and making a workable area, proceeded to shape and semi-hollow one side of the root to form a crude but effective shovel.

HOME AKIE

The weather became colder and the wind coming up the Akie at night, was chilling to the bone. It became necessary to keep improving the root structure that the two men had crawled into on the first night. The once mighty tree, lying high on the gravel bank of the meandering river, offered an immense root cave.

A decade of spring run-off had sand blasted the dirt and fibres from the base of this water-fallen giant. Sheer greatness of the tree prevented the annual surge from floating it down the water course. Gravel and large amounts of driftwood lay against the upstream side of the large root system of the aged sweeper, leaving a natural hole at the base, which was facing toward the steadfast flowing water. Small logs and driftwood railing had been put in place on the downstream side of the shelter to deflect a part of the upstream wind always seeking a way into the men's quarters, warmed by the large driftwood signal fire. Reflecting light from the tall root overhang that constituted a large part of the sanctuary's ceiling, left a glowing warmth on the wilderness campsite.

The shovels would be used first to dig further into the dirt below the wood root, making the base deeper. The indent against the tree base now became a viable shelter from the wind and cold that would become the two men's constant companion. Driftwood and dirt was fitted to the sides of the old root, making the survival hovel a simple but protecting home. The floor of the native haven was covered with spruce boughs gathered from the nearby forest.

A fire built at the entrance of the root house kept out the cold and any other unwanted intruders. It also served as a constant source of flame that would be needed in case the temporary dwelling had to become a daylight signal fire. Jim had indicated that fresh spruce boughs should be placed on the floor every day, but the drying ones were to be left in place. If a search plane was heard, a few burning embers from the blaze would instantly inflame the drying spruce boughs into a tower of flame and black smoke, curling out past the tilted ceiling of the old root abode.

Once the sanctuary was completed, Jim and Jack decided to make a pact to quit smoking, right after they finished the last Export A that Jack had saved for this moment. It was while the cherished cigarette was being smoked that the two men discussed their predicament. Good news, they were okay. No one was hurt. From there it went downhill. The secrecy surrounding the trip resulted in misinformation being given. It was indicated that the pilot and passenger were flying out for an extended trip to the Akie River.

Unless someone from Anderson's lodge at Pink Mountain had made the mile trip to Sikanni Chief flight strip and noticed that the grub stake was still in Jimmy's new 65 Oldsmobile 98, they would have guessed wrong, believing the gold-hungry, inquisitive pair had already left for a week on the commanding expedition. After that, it would be a day or two wondering if the prospectors had just needed more time — nine days — as long as winter didn't hit at that time with a week or two of unflyable weather.

It was a long time between meals, and the last one of spaghetti and meatballs, delicious as it was, had long since been dissipated by the hungry stomachs of the two men. Welcomed as the pound of ground coffee was, Jack watched with concern the tasty warmth meagrely being boiled in the container of the previous meal. He wondered about the history of the camp coffee packed in paper covered aluminum foil which was, with an axe, carefully chopped open by Jim. The solidness of the delicacy was okay with the seasoned prospector as eventually the chunks of coffee would dissolve. What bothered Jack more was that the inseparable tinfoil dissolved before the fine grind.

Flowing from the west side of the same mountain range that gathered the easterly head waters of the Prophet River, the Akie water course rushed through troughs cut by glaciers thousands of years ago. Leaving a ribbon of water winding through the Mile High Rocky Mountain divide to tumble into the Finlay River feeding Lake Williston which lay behind the massive W.A.C. Bennet Dam on the once mighty Peace River. With unknown weather patterns at this time of year the Akie water shed would be a large area to search. The two men could be stranded on the isolated river for quite some time.

Jim said, "Jack, we have to right that plane, and fly her out of here. I have checked it over and the Savage survived the river landing not bad, but I have to get the plane out of the river this fall. The winter ice will crush the wings and fuselage." Jim knew spring run-off would wash the pulverized parts of the Jackpine Savage downstream like so many pieces of driftwood floating among the rapids of the Akie River. "If the Savage can be righted and fixed, this bar, although shorter than the one we touched down on, can be made into a flight strip. If we move the big rocks to make a narrow runway, I know we can lift her out of here," Jim said with conviction.

Prospector Jack looked the veteran pilot in the eyes and saw the determined look on his weather-beaten face. He tried to fathom how they were going to get the aircraft back on its landing gear and then try to get a water-logged engine to pull the battered monoplane back into the air from a crudely built launching area. However, after he and Jimmy had finished the cigarette, Jack really didn't have a hell of a lot to do, so he looked at the bush pilot once again and said, "What do you have on your mind, Jim?"

"First thing is to remove that prop," replied the grounded pilot.

SAVAGE RESTORATION

Taking turns on the propeller removal, the icy Akie chased the frigid workers shivering from the waist-deep water, to the raging fire that warmed them. Working with their hands a foot under water, one hand held a cone-shaped rock that came crashing down on a chilled handle of the small wrench. The first of the six bolts attaching the propeller to the engine was loosened. Jimmy was always aware of the greedy current constantly striving to wrangle away essential bolts, or tugging the throbbing crescent from his water-petrified fingers. The eight inch crescent wrench was continually saved by a boot lace from Jack's hiking boots. One end tied through the hole in the implements handle, the other attached to Jimmy's wrist.

Once the prop was removed, and inspected closely by Jimmy, the two men were back in the water with the bush-made shovels, moving rock and sand from the fore part of the Savage. But as the sediment was moved from the nose of the aircraft, the current would rush in more silt to level the disturbed river bottom. It was decided the water had to be diverted.

The dike was made of larger stone twenty feet upstream from the resting Savage. This prevented the swift-moving water from backfilling the man made indents. The water streamed by the river side of the dike. Rock and sand was mucked into the flow, washing the debris away downstream. The hole got deeper, but soon the shovels became useless. Upraise movement from the five foot hole washed the material off of the inadequate tool. It looked as if the operation had come to a standstill.

The hole under the front of the aircraft had to be about seven feet deep for the nose of the Savage to flip under the wings and put the aircraft right side up. Jim looked at the equipment on the beach, and spotted the irregular cut plyboard that had been used for a freight board. Using the screwdriver, he started punching two rows of holes about four inches apart down the centre of the wood. He laid the handle of the shovel on the plywood and proceeded to stitch the spruce pole to the three foot length of plyboard. On each bottom corner of the wide end of the plyboard, he put a hole 4" up and 3" in. Next he inserted the three eighth inch rope through the first corner hole around the backside of the plywood. A clove hitch was wrapped around the 4" shovel pole and poked out the opposite corner hole. Rope was continuously fed through until an equal length came from each puncture.

This bush implement worked along the lines of a scraper. One man would pull on the two ropes protruding from the base of the straight-edged tool, while his partner directed the amount removed by tilting the handle forward for more of the river bed, or back if the plough-boy had too big of a load to pull. When the removed fill reached the dike edge, the fast-flowing current washed it away.

Flipping the plane would be tricky, but not impossible. The wings were about centre of balance, so as the nose went deeper in the river crevice, the tail went higher into the air. Standing in 18 inches of current swirling from behind the rock dike, built on the shallow outcropping upstream from the man-dug pit, Jim threw the length of 3/8" strand over his right shoulder and grabbed the tail of the rope with his left hand from behind. With his gnarled right hand he reached up towards the end of the longer length of the cut line that had (by carefully standing on wing edge) been attached to the tail section of the aircraft, now high in the air. Using his buzz saw deformed hand he wrapped the rope twice around the lean muscled arm and grabbed the hemp to best overcome the absence of his pinky finger. Seeing Prospector Jack ready and in position on the gravel bar where the elevated tail section once laid, Jim braced his frigid boot-covered foot on the rough water diversion and yelled, "Pull!!!"

Standing on the edge of the man made pit the big prospector grabbed the rope attached to the submerged cowling on the front of the aircraft. Bracing his feet on the side, Jack pulled with all his might. Both men strained to maximum strength, the downed craft slowly began a watery somersault and the nose of the Jackpine Savage finally passed under the wing span. The tail section became perpendicular at that point and the small tire on the tail of the standard landing gear came over

SAVAGE RESTORATION

centre to come crashing down into the waters of the Akie River.
The plane, now upright, was held onto the rocky river

bottom by the weight of the water which was steadily pouring from the porous fabric surrounding the wing structure and as the dissipating water made the Savage lighter, the excited men pushed with all their might on the fragile craft and with shear exertion propelled the Super Cub onto the beach, upright and still intact. The river ruined Jackpine Savage, wings drooping like a water beaten bird, solidly perched on over size tandem bush tires, sat on the banks of the Akie river.

THE HUNT

It was the fourth morning. Jack woke up a bit hungry, but nothing like the second and third day. The chill of the regular water immersion numbed the hunger pangs that occasionally racked his body. Amazingly enough, although he was being constantly exposed to the elements, his health was not noticeably suffering. The annoying cough he had seemed to clear up a couple of days after he had quit his last Export. The excess roll around his waist did not seem to hinder his movement so much as when he started three days ago dragging that damn piece of plywood through the Akie River bed. The leg muscles, although sore and sometimes stiff in the morning, were quickly becoming hard. Although he and Jim were still in good shape, the cold and hard work was wearing dangerously low on stored energy. They would soon be noticing the effects of no nourishment.

The prospector was at the far end of the gravel bar doing his habitual morning constitution when he noticed the movement downstream about one-half mile. Jack's eyes darted momentarily to the log where he had carefully set the 357 Magnum. The 357 had become his close friend. In the freshly fallen snow yesterday morning, less than fifteen feet from the root shelter, Jack had found tracks of a grizzly.

Survival gear was now carried on their hips and the men

made a point of marking out their camp area as nature called. A smirk came to Jack's lips as he recalled the pile of droppings left behind last night by someone who didn't really seem too concerned about the camp area boundaries. Judging by the size of tracks and excrement, Jack was not really interested in trying to enforce territorial law with only the help of his inadequate friend, the 357. Slowly he buttoned the front of his Levis, eyes straining to watch the spot where something had caught his attention. There it was again.

EARLY WINTER

Matriarch was moving briskly on the trail that followed the river through the rocky valley. The heavy frost had hindered her group from moving freely on the slippery rocky shores. Warming the earth enough to thaw the clustered ice, the rays of the fall sun now made it safe to travel. She sensed winter was coming early to the mountain range that her herd used as their summer feeding grounds, regrettably they left the tasty mountain foliage. Matriarch was concerned for the safety of her family. The sudden freezing had reminded her ancient instinct to move to lower levels to feed, or face the possibility of a snowbound starvation. She realized the dangers of an early winter in the mountains, soon overtaken by harsh storms and stealth wolves running across the hardened snow crust. Wolves had brought down her eldest daughter last winter. Matriarch knew how deadly heavy snows could be in the mountains.

FIRE

In the spring Matriarch had led her family to an area where the unseasonably early hot summer air had drifted through the tall grasses and low shrubs, robbing precious moisture from the already tinder-dry vegetation. A flash appeared in the heavens, followed by a tremendous crashing sound, as if a thousand trees had fallen in one instant. Thereafter a fire started in the grass for no reason at all. A very tall spruce tree was severed, as if a giant set of antlers had ripped it and from its bark a wisp of smoke issued, a little fire would start, and before long the entire forest was ablaze. Then all the grassy steppe erupted into flame.

At such moments, and Matriarch had survived two such fires in her years, the moose had learned to head for the nearest river and submerge themselves to their eye level, keeping the wide nostrils on the long nose above water for air.

When the fire was totally dead in all parts, Matriarch kept her herd close to the burned-over areas, for the moose had learned that rather quickly after such a conflagration, the roots of tenacious plants whose visible growth had been burned off enhanced the production of new shoots, thousands of them, and these were the finest food the moose ever found.

What was even more important, ashes from the great fires fertilized the ground, making it more nutritious so that the young trees would grow with a rigor they would otherwise not have known. One of the best things that could happen to the moose steppe, with its mixture of trees and grass, was to have a periodic fire of great dimension, for in its aftermath, grasses, shrubs, trees and animals prospered. It was puzzling that something as dangerous as fire, which Matriarch had twice barely escaped, should be the agency whereby she and her successors would grow strong. She did not try to solve this riddle. She protected herself and her family from the dangers and luxuriated in the rewards.

These rewards were obvious as the sleek old cow led her well-fed followers once again from the high mountain ranges. A grandson born two springs ago would soon drift away from the small herd, but for now he was content to follow the lead of the wise cow as they had browsed on the tender buds growing in abundance on the native mountain terrain.

Matriarch was leading her herd upstream with the wind so she had no chance to scent the strange smells happening. Her first alert to danger was a flash of fire followed by a large explosion, not unlike the sound that set the steppe ablaze. This sound repeated, a flash was seen coming from an animal much the size of a large wolf walking on its hind legs. Confused, Matriarch looked for the consuming flames. The wolf-like animals looked dangerous but there was no escaping from a mad dash straight into a fire, nor did she prefer the river and the chance the wolves would swim alongside, grabbing her by the tender nostrils or keep her from climbing back up the bank until she was too weak to swim or fight. The reverberating thunder bouncing back from the rocky cliffs on the other bank of the Akie, convinced Matriarch to keep heading upstream away from the noise and confusion. Followed by all but her sleek-muscled grandson.

Curious about the delay of her grandson, Matriarch returned to the river bank and watched from darkened cover the fire that should have devoured the woodland. However, these strange creatures seemed to control it and have no fear as they sat next to the flickering light. Wandering back into the safety of the forest, instinct told her that her grandson was no more and to move onto the easier accessible food in the lower valleys.

Jack arose early on the fifth day feeling well fed. Once again, he stoked up the fire in front of the airtight shanty. The bright glowing embers leapt immediately to flame, stretching its fiery fingers again towards the cooling embers embedded in the sloping root ceiling of the sleeping quarters.

The first rays of the red sunrise bounced from the tops of the upstream rapids, past the fire and streamed down from the smoky coloured ceiling. The sun light exposed the greyed charcoaled spots that had recently been gleaming embers

Home
A•Kī´ē

radiating from the heat of the night fire, lighting up the camp area with a starlight effect.

The pacifying sounds of the river gently lapping at the banks and protruding river rock was overpowered last night by the guttural sounds of tearing meat of the newly acquired feast being devoured, drifted across the darkened water. Jimmy laid listening with interest until the long hours of the day, combined with the high wood flame that the burly prospector insisted on tonight, took its toll. The comforting meal on a very thankful stomach had the worn pilot bunching his leather fleece-lined flight jacket into a pillow. Settling down in the thick Spruce bough bed, Jim stated, "May as well stretch out for the night Buds. That fire will last well into morning. From the noise coming upstream, sounds as if all the action will be down river tonight." To Jack's amazement, the contented bush pilot then closed his eyes, and went into a relaxed sleep.

The prospector had been up many times during the night to feed the fire. Now he left the dwelling to gather more firewood a short distance away. He glanced once again downstream, beyond where the meat had been hoisted, to ascertain if the two men's feasting companion was full and sleeping off the recent binge of gluttony. It had been a cold star-bright night, but the flame had not been necessarily kept high because of the chill. The huge fire at the entrance had kept the wood and earth home at a more than comfortable temperature.

.Breakfast steak would soon be sliced from the hind quarter that hung some hundred yards distance from the fire and dwelling, suspended ten feet above the gravel bar by three eighth inch rope firmly attached to the leg bone and the other rope end to a discarded tree which was protruding from a giant pile of pick-up sticks. Endless swelling current brought more logs to the unruly pile each spring.

FLIGHT PREPARATION

Today they would be checking the oil and fuel of the Savage. The versed pilot had switched the fuel cocks off just after the inverted Jackpine Savage had been beached, so the polluted fuel could not reach the gas lines or the carburettor of the Lycoming engine. The wing tanks and the motor had been submerged in water for the better part of four days. Condensation as well as possible engine leaks would cause the aircraft motor to immediately seize from the unwanted liquid. The petroleum products would have to be purified.

For this they needed a container. Being the only metal container other than the coffee can (now being used only to heat water) the quart oil can was promptly opened and the precious fluid, which would be used to top up the unknown amount of oil loss in the motor, was poured into one of the plastic vomit bags and set carefully into a sand and gravel mould so the unobtainable liquid would not spill.

The solid tin oil can was then placed under the engine drain plug and using the crescent wrench to remove the plug, the oil was drained into the can until the quart was full. Water was removed by pouring the lubrication back into the motor until the bottom of the can contained only water, which was then dumped unceremoniously on the banks of the Akie River.

The gas in the wing tanks had been contaminated by the water of the tributary. Using the fuel switches on the left tank to regulate the gas flow, the gas was drained one quart at a time, from the port tank and poured into the right wing tank, the debased liquid in the bottom of the tin being discarded. This continued until the left wing tank was emptied. Two cans of recovered gas were reintroduced to the port fuel tank and thoroughly sloshed about. Then, redraining the two quarts of fluid, and finding no water in this last operation, it was decided the tank was purified.

It was now time to do the same thing with the right tank, only there would be twice as much fluid to separate. One quart at a time, the fuel in the starboard tank was defouled as it was conveyed to the unsoiled port wing tank. When emptied, the purging of the right wing tank took place. Half the fuel in the left tank was then poured back into the right tank to equal the weight as close as possible for the critical takeoff. This also allowed one more discriminating check for purity of the high octane aviation gas in the starboard lift-off tank.

On the sixth day, Jack found out why Jim had been studying the prop. It had been slightly bent in the initial turnover of the Savage and would have to be straightened. The vibrations from the untrue prop would shake the Savage apart long before the engine of the bush plane reached the 3600 R.P.M. needed for takeoff. Discouraged, the weather-beaten prospector could see the problem. Without tools it didn't seem as if the damaged prop could be used.

Jack thought of the days spent in the waist-deep water righting the Savage, then the many hours purging the wing fuel tanks and separating the impurities from the refined petroleum products stored in the wings and motor of the Jackpine Savage. Although, the plane was now safe on the gravel bar until spring run-off, and the grub had become a lot better since he and Jim had brought down the young bull moose with the survival hardware. Jack was still a little disappointed that after all that labour, the marooned men were not going to lift off from the narrow, diminutive, flight strip that had been partly constructed on the stunted gravel bar. It now seemed it would be used only as winter camp for the Jackpine Savage.

The large prospector was getting cabin fever from the cramped living accommodations under the old root. The moose herd moving upstream from the high Muskwa Mountain Range only confirmed his belief that it was getting very close to winter settling in. Rescue, he felt, was about due. But with winter snows and fog close at hand, moose could be the main staple for a bit longer.

Jimmy however, had other ideas. He grabbed the two axes, and carried them over to an alder at the edge of the grove. It's trunk had split at about 3 feet above ground. The pilot placed the cutting edge of one axe about six inches up from the split crotch of the tree. Using the other axe as a hammer he proceeded to chisel out a notch about four inches deep on the inside sections of the tree.

The prop was then slipped into these notches and the two-bladed propeller was held vise-like straight out parallel with the rugged terrain. Looping the rope around the twin forks three feet above the split trunk, a sturdy piece of driftwood was then stuck vertically through the two wraps of rope. Turning the wooden lever in a clockwise direction twisted the rope. The two trunks were drawn together as the shrinking rope span knotted up, welding the alloy prop to the compressed fibres of the aged growth.

With one pole on each side of the high pitched propeller, the shovels were then securely lashed in a 'T' fashion to the free end of the prop.

The pressure applied by the men to straighten the prop was critical. Although the fixed-pitch propeller had just brushed the huge Akie River rock that flipped the Savage, it had twisted and bent the craft puller ever so slightly. With the seasoned eye of a pilot who had straightened the occasional prop, Jim cautioned the muscular prospector on using too much force on the leverage supplied by the shovel handles. The two men firmly pressed down on their section of the poles attached to the presently useless sculptured alloy. Jack's side needed a bit more force as the twist had to be put back into the prop. The downward pressure, regulated by Jim's knowing eye, slowly straightened the diminutive bend in the badly needed propeller. Unceremoniously, the two-bladed prop was attached and the six bolts hammered on tightly with the cone-shaped river rock striking the handle of the eight inch crescent wrench.

LIFE TO THE SAVAGE

The battery had survived the landing, and although upside down, a small ball in each cell of the airplane energy unit immediately went to the air vent in the cell cap preventing any loss of acid. The stored electricity was merely a convenience, as the Lycoming motor would fire up by turning the under eight-foot prop by hand, exciting the magneto, which in turn would fire the spark plugs exploding the pistons to life.

However the magnetos were as wet as the spark plugs that sat upside down under water for the better part of four days. These water-logged electrical devices, each feeding their bank of four plugs, had to be dry. Shortage of tools dictated that the cramped generators would not be dried by temporarily removing them from the heart of the uprighted Savage. The long handled flat head screwdriver would not fit between the magneto and fire wall of the aircraft. The back plates of the magnetos were removed by using the pliers and a dime to fit into the flat-headed screws holding the backing plates in place.

Hot rocks were then placed from the fire into the empty quart oil can that had been used for purging the fuel. The can was held with pliers up to the exposed rear of the dampened mag and with puffs from the tire pump, warm air whisked away the moisture from the delicate ignition points.

Removal of the spark plugs proved to be challenging. The method that decidedly worked best was by tapping the back of one axe with another, the tip of the first axe simulating a cold chisel slowly worked the plug loose, thus removing all eight plugs from the horizontally opposed Lycoming motor.

HOME WARD BOUND

The spark plugs were laid out on the warm rocks. The fire flickered drying flame over the impending ignition spark which would ignite the vapours of the aviation gas, in the four cylinders of the 150 H.P. engine.

Pulling down on one side of the reconditioned propeller, the water-logged cylinder walls were wiped clean as the watery fluid ejected from the bottom spark plug holes. Fire crisp spark igniters were then inserted back into the dual holed cylinder heads. Portside generator spark plug wires were then connected to the top bank. The starboard magneto served the bottom four spark plugs. Several downward pulls on the over seven foot aluminum alloy prop and the 150 H.P. Lycoming engine coughed and sputtered. Then in an instant the Jackpine Savage roared to life!

HOMEWARD

Matriarch lifted her head towards the aircraft noise thundering down from the heavens which sent the old cow's younger daughter and its heifer into a brief run. Seeing only the outline of a huge bird, much like the large eagles that fished the northern river, she continued feeding. These loud predators posed her no danger.

The grandmother moose would not have understood that the men flying the bird were alive and well because of the sacrifice of the young bull. If Matriarch's memory of her descendant had not faded so fast or if the warming winds had lured her and her small herd of five once again to the mountain foliage, she might have wandered downstream towards the gravel flight strip.

She would not have understood why the two beings she felt were responsible for her offspring's demise wrestled with large river rocks, eventually climbed into the gigantic bird, and flew off of the gravel bar from which she had watched the flickering firelight. The old cow moose would not have comprehended the landing of the super cub on an old strip midway to its destination to dump the contaminated fuel from the sediment bowl, which was three-quarters full of the lethal river water. Arriving home thirty minutes later just in time to stop a search and rescue plan initiated by the clearing weather and calls of assistance from the search centre, Anderson's Pink Mountain Lodge, Mile 147 on the Alaska Highway.

Matriarch gave grunts of encouragement as her family gorged themselves on the drying vegetation, storing as much fuel as possible for the coming winter. The wise old cow had learned that the survival of their species did not depend very much on the great males with their tremendous showy antlers and brazen challenges. The males appeared only in mid-fall for the mating period. The rest of the year they were nowhere to be seen.

Matriarch, the grandmother cow moose in obedience to the instinct of her species, took responsibility for rearing, protecting and educating the young, whom the survival of her race, ultimately depended on.

March 1, 1993

Dear Jamie,

With reference to our recnt telephone conversation I am enclosing a draft contribution to the book that you are writing about your Dad. Please go over it with your Dad and feel free to edit it or change it in any way you wish. If you would like help from me please contact me. I am looking forward to meeting you. Please tell your Dad to stop in when he is in Dawson Creek.

Kindest regards.

Mr. Levis presently serves as a
Provincial Court Judge of British Columbia

A JUDGE'S ANECDOTE

*O*n November 1963, I arrived in Fort St. John, B.C. with my wife and family, to carry on the practice of law.

I did not meet Jim for some considerable time after my arrival in the north country. I had heard many stories about the courageous and heroic deeds carried out by the bush pilots who lived in the area. These daring and valiant men with their machines were always available in emergent situations. They would fly their aircraft in conditions that an ordinary pilot would consider impossible, in order to bring help and assistance to a person or persons in need. The bush pilot whom I would hear the most stories about was 'Midnight Anderson' as Jim was often called.

I did not know that when we would meet, Jim would bring into my office the most memorable case of my career.

I still remember the day Jim and I first met. It was a warm sunny day in the spring of 1964. He attended my office dressed in blue jeans, blue jean shirt, cowboy boots, and wearing a cowboy hat with one side of the brim folded upward. He had a round weathered face and bright blue eyes that sparkled when he smiled and laughed. He would squint and blink his eyes as he talked.

Jim pulled out of his back pocket some documents that obviously he had been carrying there for some time. I skimmed through these papers, and noted that one of the documents referred to a court action against Jim, claiming the return of an aircraft, and another document related to the seizure of the aircraft by the Sheriff. I asked Jim to tell me the

CAPTURING CRAFTS

circumstances as to how he became involved in this lawsuit. What he told me kept me glued to my chair in amazement.

A zoologist owned a game farm near Edmonton, Alberta. He had entered into a contract with the federal game department to cross domesticated reindeer from the Canadian Arctic, with wild Caribou in order to produce a larger hybrid reindeer, for meat utilization in the Arctic.

The zoologist came to the Pink Mountain area, and hired a hunting guide to catch calf caribou for this project. When the young caribou reached maturity his intention was to then cross-breed the animals. The hunting guide hired by the zoologist hunted the calves on horseback, and after fourteen days the guide caught one small caribou calf.

Jim knew about this project and kept track of the efforts of the hunting guide. He felt that this method of catching caribou would not be successful. Jim approached the zoologist and told him that he could catch adult caribou for him. The zoologist looked at Jim with scepticism and asked how he would accomplish that.

Jim told him that he would haze the animals into nets, and deliver them to the game farm in Edmonton. It would advance the hybrid project by about four years. Interested, the

zoologist then asked Jim what he would charge for an adult caribou. Jim answered that it would be $1,000.00 per head, the same amount a hunting guide would charge to shoot one dead.

The zoologist, still very sceptical about Jim's proposal finally said to him "bring me one". At that time Jim did not have his own aircraft. He borrowed a Piper Cub aircraft from a friend. Levelling an area on top of Klingzut Mountain so he could land and take off, Jim and crew with out delay set up nets on that mountain top. He then took off in the aircraft and as he described it, "flying six feet off the rocks I hazed the caribou into the nets". Landing and trussing up the caribou,he loaded it into the back seat area of the aircraft flew to Anderson's lodge, and then transported the mature caribou to the zoologist's game farm by truck. Jim's arriving at the game farm gate with an adult caribou in tow, unquestionably impressed the zoologist.

The zoologist told Jim that he wanted twenty adult caribou and six Rocky Mountain stone sheep, and that he would obtain the permits necessary to take these animals. Jim told him he was presently without an aircraft, and that he would have to have one.

The zoologist agreed to buy an aircraft. Jim told him it had to be a Piper cub aircraft, outfitted with tandem balloon tires for landing and taking off on the mountain top. The Zoologist supplied the aircraft and Jim went to work.

It took Jim several months to complete his task. He caught all animals in the same manner as has been described. On one occasion as Jim was flying back to his home with a caribou, it came loose and started thrashing about. He landed on the Alaska Highway and flagged down a car full of American tourists. He told them that he had a caribou in the back of his aircraft, and needed help to tie it up. The tourists agreed to help but approaching the aircraft they heard the animal thrashing about, and quickly returned to their car and left.

One of the animals was so large it could not fit into the aircraft. Jim had a Bombardier type tracked vehicle upon which he built a cage. That animal was transported off the mountain by this vehicle.

After delivering all animals to the Zoologist's game farm Jim did not hear from him. However, Jim was quite happy to have the aircraft. Jim's life was flying, and this aircraft was new and outfitted for his type of flying. When he was served with the documents and the aircraft seized, Jim understandably became very upset and came to me.

I advised Jim that he should immediately bring his own action against the zoologist for a debt owing of $26,000.00, representing the value of catching 26 animals at $1,000.00 per head. I also advised Jim that an application should be made to the court to consolidate this new action, with the action brought against him for the return of the aircraft. This was done and we then waited for the trial date.

The law suit was to be tried by a Supreme Court judge, making it necessary to wait for the Supreme Court assizes, which occurred only twice a year in those days. The court sittings took place in Pouce Coupe,B.C., and all matters proceeding to a trial or hearing in the Peace River region, would be set for trial at those two sittings. We were heading for the

TEMPORARY CAMP

spring sitting which was scheduled for the month of April, so we had several months to wait.

The zoologist and his game farm being located in Alberta gave me concern about collecting the money if we were successful. As long as the aircraft remained in British Columbia it could be returned to Jim if we won the case. I was served with a notice that an application was going to be made before a judge in Prince George, B.C. asking for an order that the aircraft be returned to the Zoologist in Alberta.

Immediately I contacted Jim to advise that we had to try and oppose the application. I agreed to meet Jim at my house the day before the application was set to be heard so that we could drive to Prince George, stay overnight and then attend the hearing the next morning.

Jim arrived at my home and instead of driving to Prince

PERMANENT CAMP

George, suggested that we fly in a Piper Cub aircraft, that he had borrowed from one of his friends. I had not flown with Jim up to this time, and told him that I preferred to drive. He persisted that we should fly. Seeing that it was a beautiful sunny calm day, I gave in and agreed to fly. As soon as I agreed to fly, Jim made a telephone call and enquired whether he could land in Prince George by using lights, or whether the air traffic there was controlled by radio. When I asked Jim why he had made that enquiry, he replied that the earphones for the radio were left at Pink Mountain, but he knew a place where we could land.

We drove to a farmers field where the Piper Cub aircraft was parked. I got in and worked the fuel feed lever while Jim hand-cranked the propeller, starting the engine. He climbed in and we were off to Prince George. My pilot's licence recently acquired, it did not take very long for me to realize the superior skills of Jim as a pilot. I sat back and enjoyed a beautiful trip across the Rocky Mountains.

Approaching Prince George Jim reduced his altitude, I noticed that he was constantly looking down and around. I suspected that he did not know a field where we could land, but was in the process of finding one. We flew over the city and along the Nechako River. Suddenly he pointed to an area and said that there was a field where we could land. I looked and saw a small clearing bordered by tall trees. Knowing that I would not be able to land safely in such a small area, it was quite inspiring to set down, and use only half of the clearing before we came to a stop.

The area where we landed was rather isolated and I asked Jim how we were going to get into town. He replied that we would walk out to the road, not far from the field, and hitch-hike into town.

There I was dressed in my suit carrying my brief case, with Jim in his usual blue jeans, cowboy boots and hat, standing on the gravel road. A car came along travelling from Prince George and Jim flagged it down. The occupant was a man on his way home from work. Jim told this man that he had just landed an aircraft in a nearby field, and needed a ride into town. He had to arrange with Prince George airport to use lights instead of radio to land. The man looked at us in disbelief, and after considerable hesitation said that he would drive us into town, but first he wanted to see the airplane. We took him to the location of the aircraft and then he drove us into town.

Driving along, Jim went into more detail explaining why it was necessary for him to obtain permission, to land at the airport using lights instead of radio. He also explained to the man the nature of our business, that had brought us to Prince George. After listening to Jim the man said that he had a son who had just graduated from high school, and as a reward for him he asked Jim if he would fly his son over to the airport, if he was able to get permission to land there. Jim agreed to this request, the man dropped us off at our hotel, and went to pick up his son.

CAMP MASCOT

Jim made the arrangements to land at the airport, and the man with his son picked up Jim and I. We drove back to the aircraft where Jim and the man's son took off for the airport. The man and I then drove to collect them.

Later that evening, the man returned to the hotel and the three of us spent some time in the hotel lounge. The man was so grateful to Jim for giving his son the flight in the aircraft, that neither Jim nor I could spend any money in the lounge.

The next morning we attended court. I was not successful in opposing the application to keep the aircraft in British Columbia until the conclusion of the trial. As a result I was concerned about collecting the judgement if Jim was successful. All we could do was wait for the trial and its outcome.

About ten days before the Supreme Court assizes was to begin, I received word that this trial was number three on the list and that I should be ready to proceed on a certain date. I contacted Jim and told him to be ready to proceed with our witnesses on that specific date.

On the day the Supreme Court Judge arrived from Vancouver, I received word that the two trials scheduled before mine had collapsed due to last minute settlements. The Judge had ordered my trial to proceed at ten o'clock the next morning. I knew that I was going to have difficulty locating Jim, to advise him that he must be in the Pouce Coupe court house by ten o'clock the next morning. I knew also that Jim was going to find it difficult to round up his witnesses because they were located in isolated areas, with no access to a telephone.

I finally made contact with Jim and advised him of the developments, and he immediately started to fly about trying to locate his witnesses. I told him to try and get to the courthouse by ten o'clock, but felt that we did not have sufficient notice for Jim to be there on time.

I arrived at the court house early on the morning of the trial day; April 7, 1965, to await the arrival of Jim and our witnesses. I met the Judge and welcomed him to the Peace river country, I could tell that he was not happy being in Pouce Coupe at this time of the year. The weather was miserable with cold wet snow, and mud conditions. The motel where the Judge stayed did not have a restaurant, and he told me that when he walked to the nearest coffee shop for breakfast, he had his rubbers "sucked off twice in the mud".

It was approximately nine o'clock and Jim had not arrived. I explained to the Judge that my client may not arrive by ten o'clock, because of the short notice advising me that the trial date had moved ahead two days. Also, I told the Judge that some of the witnesses lived in isolated areas along the Alaska

Highway and did not have telephones, and my client was flying about to notify them to be here. His reply was that the trial will begin at ten sharp. Fortunately the case was consolidated in such a way, that the zoologist remained as the claimant and was required to proceed first. The trial started without Jim being present so he was unable to hear the beginning of the zoologist's evidence. Jim did arrive after the lunch break, just before the proceedings resumed and I of course was very happy to see him.

For Jim's case I proceeded by calling him as my first witness. Jim is a soft spoken person and the Judge kept telling him in an abrupt manner to speak up. Jim had never been involved in a court case, and because of the abruptness of the Judge he became flustered and had difficulty giving his evidence. I felt my case was off to a rocky start. However, as the trial proceeded and Jim explained how he caught these animals, the Judge's disposition seemed to mellow and Jim's case proceeded smoothly from that point onward.

The basis for the Zoologist's case was that he had never agreed to pay $1,000.00 per animal, and that a reasonable value per animal would be no more than $100.00. Also, it was his position that he had supplied equipment to Jim, the value of which exceeded $2,600.00, and he therefore was not indebted to Jim at all.

One of my witnesses gave evidence that he had met the Zoologist at a dining establishment along the Alaska Highway, and at that time they discussed the Zoologist's project. The witness said that in the part of the discussion regarding the catching of the animals, the Zoologist told him that he was paying Jim $1,000.00 for each animal. Also, one of my witnesses, a hunting guide, gave evidence that his charge to a hunter for a caribou hunt was $1,000.00 , and the same amount was a reasonable price for the work carried out by Jim.

At the conclusion of the three day trial the Judge said that

JIMMY

he wanted to take some time to consider the evidence, and the court would adjourn for approximately one hour. When the court reconvened, the Judge rendered a verdict in favour of Jim for the full amount of his claim. Both Jim and I were very pleased with the result. The Zoologist was not so pleased and he instructed his lawyer to launch an appeal. The appeal was successful only to the extent that the trial judge had failed to make an allowance, for the use of the aircraft owned and supplied by the Zoologist. We agreed that the award should be reduced, and an amount was agreed to by both sides. The award was reduced accordingly.

The next step in the proceedings for Jim and I was to collect the amount owing to Jim on the final judgement. The Zoologist did not own any assets in British Columbia that could be seized and sold to satisfy the judgement. Jim could sue the Zoologist in the province of Alberta on the basis of the B.C. judgement but that was an expensive procedure.

The Zoologist would periodically travel to places within British Columbia to give lectures and show slides of the animals located in his game farm. I received word that he was in Fort Nelson, B.C. on such a tour. I immediately prepared seizure documents relating to his station wagon motor vehicle and instructed the Sheriff to seize it.

I received a call from the Sheriff in Fort Nelson advising me that he had located the station wagon but it contained the Zoologist's pet Cheetah, and he was not going to seize that. I told him to place a seizure notice on the vehicle, and to tell the Zoologist that the vehicle or its contents would not be released until the Sheriff received authority from me.

Shortly after that call I received a call from the Zoologist. In our discussion we entered into an agreement whereby I would authorize the Sheriff to release the station wagon, and a draft for the total amount owing to Jim would be in my office on or before a certain date. I authorized the release of the automobile, and the Zoologist was good on his word. That ended the case.

During these court proceedings, Jim and I became good friends. My wife and I and children would on occasion visit Jim at his home at Pink Mountain. Besides being an excellent pilot and outdoors man, he was also an artist. His home was decorated with murals of northern scenes often containing animals burnt into slabs of wood. Outside his porch is a rain barrel painted red with the inscription 'pure swamp water - not a moose turd in it'.

When speaking of people who are the salt of the earth, Jim is certainly one of those persons and a true northerner as well. Representing him in his lawsuit was truly an unforgettable experience.

If I'd known I was going to live this long, I would have taken better care of myself.

Health restored and living at the base of Pink Mountain on the Alaska highway, retired Jimmy Anderson frequently discusses rebuilding a retrieved bush broken super cub, to once again pilot the Jackpine Savage skyward.